Ski
1979

An Opening Repertoire
for the
Attacking Club Player

An Opening Repertoire
for the
Attacking Player

David Levy
Raymond Keene

MASON / CHARTER

New York 1977

First published 1976
© David Levy, Raymond Keene 1976

Printed in Great Britain

First published in the U.S.
by Mason/Charter Publishers, Inc.

Library of Congress Cataloging in Publication Data

Levy, David N   L
  An opening repertoire for the attacking player.

  London ed. published in 1976 under title: An
opening repertoire for the attacking club player.
    1. Chess--Openings. I. Keene, Raymond D.,
joint author. II. Title.
GV1450.L45   1977   794.1'22   76-27294
ISBN 0-88405-436-5

Contents

Symbols

+	Check
++	Double Check
±	Some advantage for White
∓	Some advantage for Black
±	Clear advantage for White
∓	Clear advantage for Black
±±	White has a won game
∓∓	Black has a won game
=	Balanced position
!	Good move
!!	Excellent move
!?	Interesting move
?!	Doubtful move
?	Inferior move
??	Losing move
1-0	Black resigned
0-1	White resigned
$\frac{1}{2}$-$\frac{1}{2}$	Draw agreed

W or *B* at the side of each diagram indicates which side is to move.

Preface

This book is written for the club player who would like to have a good command of the openings he plays but who has insufficient time to study reams of chess analysis. After a day at work it is too much to ask of a club player that he spends a couple of hours studying the latest Soviet analysis before he plays a local league match or a game in his club championship. How then should he combat the growing army of young players, schoolboys and students, who have plenty of time for home analysis and study and who *are* armed to the teeth with the very latest innovations?

The answer lies in being able to channel the game into variations that you will know better than your opponent; variations in which the theory is unlikely to change frequently and in which you feel comfortable because you have grasped the basic ideas and know sufficient theory to guarantee at least a level position when entering the middle game. With these ideas in mind the publishers have commissioned two volumes, each tailored to a different style of player. In this book we suggest a repertoire of openings that we feel will appeal to the more aggressive and dynamic club players. Bernard Cafferty's companion volume has been written for those who prefer a more positional struggle.

The openings and defences that we have chosen to offer our reader all lead to interesting sharp positions. At every stage the reader is given only one choice if it is his turn to move, but he is told how he should play against each of his opponent's plausible replies. In this way we immediately reduce to a fraction the amount of material that the reader needs to study in order to master a particular system.

The slimness of this volume will, we hope, induce the reader to make a thorough study of all our recommendations. He will then, with the minimum of effort, have learned a complete repertoire of chess openings suited to his style, which guarantee him either some advantage from the opening or, at the very least, a lively position offering chances to both sides. If the conscientious reader makes a more detailed examination of the more critical variations he will find himself scoring well from these 'roughly equal' positions through his familiarity with them.

We should like to thank Margaret Fitzjames and Jacqueline Keene-Levy for typing our manuscript and helping with the diagrams, and Kevin O'Connell for checking the typescript and reading the proofs.

RDK, DNLL
London

Introduction

This book has been tailored for those with aggressive styles and it is therefore natural that we recommend 1 P-K4 as the opening move with White. As White's main weapon we suggest the Max Lange Attack-Two Knights' Defence-Scotch Gambit complex of openings. This is to thwart opponents who are experts in the Ruy Lopez and to help the reader reach positions that are rich in tactical possibilities. The most common reply to 1 P-K4 is the Sicilian Defence with its numerous variations, some of which must be remembered to beyond move twenty by those who wish to practise them or who are likely to meet them. In order to combat all Sicilian players with one fell swoop we suggest, after 1 P-K4 P-QB4, the move 2 P-QB3 which often leads into the Smith-Morra Gambit Declined.

The Pirc Defence is of special importance to our readers. We recommend it as the defence to 1 P-K4 and of course the reader must also know how to play against the Pirc with White. For this purpose we suggest the Robert Byrne variation which leads to sharp positions that offer chances to both sides.

Against 1 P-Q4 the reader is recommended to adopt the lively Benko Gambit, while against quieter opening moves we offer lines that quickly lead to unbalanced positions.

When deciding which openings and defences to recommend to the repertoire player we were careful to ensure that transpositional possibilities could not lead to variations that we do not discuss. In fact the opposite occurs more than once. If the reader does not particularly like the system that we recommend after 1 P-K4 P-Q4 2 PxP N-KB3, he can force a transposition to the variation that we suggest against the Caro-Kann. And if, after 1 N-KB3 P-Q3, our reader's opponent should shy away from 2 P-Q4, he will transpose into one of the lines considered elsewhere in the book.

Chapters 10, 11, 16, 17 and 18 are written by Raymond Keene, the remainder by David Levy.

1 The Backbone of the Repertoire

| | 1 P-K4 P-K4 | 2 N-KB3 N-QB3 |

In this chapter we examine the Max Lange Attack, the Classical Variation of the Two Knights' Defence and a line of the Scotch Gambit that can arise if Black avoids the other two systems. These three form the most important part of our discussion of the symmetrical KP openings.

3 P-Q4

This is the best way to reach the position shown in diagram 1 because if 3 B-B4 B-B4 4 P-Q4, Black can safely play 4...B×P!

| 3... | P×P |

3...N×P 4 N×N P×N 5 Q×P leaves White with complete command of the centre and allows him much the easier development.

3...P-Q4 can be refuted by 4 N×P! N×N (or 4...P×P 5 B-QN5±) 5 P×N P×P 6 Q×Q+ K×Q 7 N-B3±

After 3...P-Q3 White can exchange on K5 and Q8 and play the semi-ending in which he has a slight advantage.

4 B-QB4(1)

We have reached the first important point of divergence and must now split this chapter into three distinct sections:

Part One: 4...B-B4

Part Two: 4...N-KB3 5 O-O N×P
Part Three: 4...N-KB3 5 O-O B-B4

4...B-N5+ 5 P-B3 P×P 6 O-O gives White a dangerous attack, akin to some variations of the dreaded Goring Gambit Accepted. e.g.

a) 6...P×P 7 B×NP N-B3 (not 7...B-B1 8 N-B3±; 7...P-B3? 8 P-K5; or 7...K-B1 8 P-K5, and in each case White has more than enough for the pawn — Keres) 8 N-N5 O-O 9 P-K5 N×P (if 9...P-Q4 10 P×N P×B 11 Q-R5! P-KR3 12 N-K4±±) 10 B×N P-Q4 11 Q-B2! P-KN3 (11...P×B loses to 12 R-Q1 followed by 13 B×N etc.) 12 B-Q3 N-N5 13 N-KB3 N×B 14 N×N Q-B3 15 P-B4 and Black's three pawns offer no match to White's extra piece. According to Keres White has a won game.

b) 6...P-Q3 7 P-QR3 B-R4 8 P-QN4 B-N3 9 Q-N3 Q-B3 10 N×P with a strong attack for the pawn — Keres.

c) 6...Q-B3 7 P-K5 P×P 8 B×NP! Q-N3 9 B-Q3 Q-K3 10 P-QR3 ± or

d) 6...P-B7 7 Q×P KN-K2 8 P-QR3± with a powerful position for White in each case.

Part One:
1 P-K4 P-K4 2 N-KB3 N-QB3 3 P-Q4 P×P 4 B-QB4

4...	B-B4
5 O-O	P-Q3

5...N-B3 6 P-K5 transposes to the Max Lange Attack (Part Three)

6 P-B3	B-KN5

After 6...P×P 7 Q-N3, a lively position is reached offering chances to both sides. e.g.:

a) 7...N-R4 8 B×P+ K-B1 9 Q×BP K×B 10 N-N5+ K-B1 11 Q×N P-KR3 12 N-KB3 N-K2 when Black has slightly the better development but his king is somewhat exposed. One possible plan for White is 13 B-K3 and if 13...B×B 14 P×B K-N1 15 N-R4 followed by N-QB3, R-B2 and QR-KB1.

b) 7...Q-Q2 (not 7...Q-B3 or 7...Q-K2, both of which can be met by 8 N×P with the unpleasant threat of 9 N-Q5.) 8 Q×BP P-B3 9 B-K3 B-N3 10 N-R3 N-K2. In return for the sacrificed pawn White has somewhat the easier game. His development is complete, Black's king is still in the centre and Black is exposed along his KN1-QR7 diagonal.

7 P-N4!

A new move. Previous theory only considered 7 Q-N3 when 7...B×N 8 B×P+ K-B1 9 P×B N-B3 10 B-KB4 P×P 11 P×P can be met by 11...N-QR4 12 Q-K6 Q-K2 13 Q×Q+ K×Q with complete equality.

7 ...   B-N3(2)

If 7...B×N 8 Q×B N-K4 9 Q-N3! Black's position is not easy. e.g.:
a) 9...N×B 10 P×B and now if 10...Q-B3 then 11 N-R3 N×N 12 B×N
PQ5×P 13 P×P P×P 14 B×P (threatening 15 B-K5), or if 10...PQ3×P 11
N-R3 N×N 12 B×N P-QN3 13 P×P Q×P (if 13...P×P? 14 Q×NP Q-B3 15
Q-B8+ ±±) 14 QR-Q1 Q-B3 15 Q×BP and Black is helpless.
b) 9...B-N3 10 B-K2 P×P (if 10...N-KB3 11 P-QR4 P-QR3 12 Q×P R-
KN1 13 Q-R6 P-Q6 14 B-Q1, Black will eventually lose his advanced
QP and his king will have trouble is finding a safe haven) 11 N×P Q-B3
12 B-N2, and White has ample compensation for the pawn.

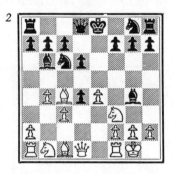

8 Q-N3	B×N
9 B×P+	K-B1
10 P×B	N-B3

If 10...N-K4 11 B×N R×B (11...N×P+?! 12 K-R1 R×N 13 N-Q2 gives
White sufficient compensation for the pawn because Black's king is the
more exposed.) 12 P-KB4! N-N5 (or 12...N-B6+ 13 K-N2 N-R5+ 14 K-
R1 when Black's knight is out of play) 13 P-B4 with a complicated
position offering White slightly the better practical chances. e.g.
13...Q-R5 14 Q-N3 Q×Q+ 15 RP×Q P-B4 16 P-B3 N-B3 17 P-K5 P×KP
18 P×KP N-Q2 19 P-K6 N-K4 20 P×P B×P 21 B-R3 P-QN3 22 B×B+
P×B 23 N-Q2 K-K2 24 P-B4 N-N5 25 P-B5 N-K6 26 R-B4.

11   B-QB4

In the variation mentioned in the note to White's seventh move, the
text would not be possible because with White's QNP at QN2 Black
could reply . . . N-QR4. Hence the point of 7 P-N4!

The present position is rather interesting. White has the advantage of
the two bishops and his king is the safer of the two. In contrast, Black
has completed his development and he has the better pawn structure.
All in all we slightly favour White's chances. The reader is strongly

urged to devote some time to a study of this position as it may be crucial for the symmetrical KP part of the repertoire.

Part Two:

1 P-K4 P-K4 2 N-KB3 N-QB3 3 P-Q4 P×P 4 B-QB4

4 ...	N-B3
5 O-O	N×P(*3*)

5...P-Q3 6 N×P B-K2 is a line that allows White too great a share of the centre as well as eventual attacking prospects against Black's K-side. e.g. 7 N-QB3 O-O (or 7...B-Q2 8 N-B5 B×N 9 P×B O-O 10 P-KN4 N-Q2 11 P-B4 N-N3 12 B-Q3±) 8 P-QN3 B-Q2 9 B-N2 R-K1 10 Q-Q2 N-K4 11 B-K2 P-B3 12 P-KB4 N-N3 13 QR-K1± (a considerable space advantage and good chances on the K-side, especially against KN7), Euwe-Geus, The Hague 1925.

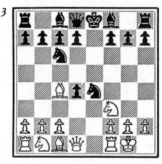

3

6 R-K1	P-Q4

6...B-K2? 7 R×N P-Q4 8 R×B+ N×R gives Black a rook and two pawns for two minor pieces but in order to attempt to retain both pawns he must tie himself up in knots: 9 B-B1! P-QB4 10 P-QN4! P-QN3 11 P×P P×P 12 B-R3 Q-B2 (or 12...Q-R4 13 Q-Q2!±) 13 P-B3 P×P 14 N×P and both Black's QP and his QBP seem to be ripe for early picking.

6...P-B4 fails at once to 7 N×P B-B4 8 R×N+! P×R 9 Q-R5+ ±±

7 B×P	Q×B
8 N-B3	

We now examine:

A 8...*Q-KR4*

B 8...*Q-Q1*

C 8...*Q-QR4*

8...Q-B5? is bad on account of 9 N-Q2! Q-R3 10 N-Q5 Q-R4 11 P-QB4! B-K3 (if 11...P×Pep 12 N-QB4!) 12 N-N3 Q-R5 13 N×BP+ K-Q1 14 N×B+ P×N 15 R×N P-K4 16 B-N5+ K-B2 17 P-B4!± Schlechter.

8...Q-KB4? is equally bad because on 9 N×N White has various ways to take advantage of the position of Black's queen, e.g. 9...B-K2 10 B-N5 O-O 11 N-N3 Q-B4 12 B×B N×B 13 Q×P±; or 9...B-K3 10 N×P N×N 11 Q×N B-K2 12 B-R6!! R-KN1 13 B-Q2 P-QR3 14 B-B3 B-B3 15 Q-R4+! P-N4 16 Q-R5± (Black is almost lost — his king is stuck in the centre and his Q-side is very weak; even ...P-QB4 is not available.) Fajarowicz-Preusse, 1932.

A

1 P-K4 P-K4 2 N-KB3 N-QB3 3 P-Q4 P×P 4 B-QB4 N-B3 5 O-O N×P 6 R-K1 P-Q4 7 B×P Q×B 8 N-B3

8 ...	Q-KR4(*4*)

9 N×N	B-K3
10 B-N5	

Preventing . . .O-O-O and temporarily shutting Black's queen out of play.

10 ...	B-QN5!

Possibly best although 10...B-Q3 also deserves some consideration. Karaklajic-Westerinen, Beverwijk 1967 then continued (10...B-Q3) 11 N×B+ P×N 12 B-B4 O-O 13 N×P Q×Q, and now 14 KR×Q leaves White with a slight plus.

Other moves are certainly inferior. e.g.

a) 10...B-K2 11 B×B N×B 12 N×P B-N5 (or 12...Q×Q 13 QR×Q O-O-O 14 N-KN5!) 13 P-KB3 B-Q2 14 Q-Q2 O-O 15 N-KB6+ ± Chigorin-Janowski, Paris 1900.

b) 10...P-KR3? (This is simply an embarrassing waste of time.) 11 B-B6! Q-R4 (or 11...Q-Q4 12 P-B3! P-Q6 13 N-Q4 N×N 14 P×N Q-QR4 15 Q×P B-N5 16 P-Q5! ±± Szabo-Muhring, Zaandam 1946) 12 N×P! P×B 13 N×P + K-K2 14 P-QN4! N×P 15 N×B! K×N 16 Q-Q4+ with a killing attack, Rossolimo-Prins, Bilbao 1951.

11 P-B3	P×P

12 P×P	B-R4

It is not clear that the bishop has a better future on any other diagonal. Shkurovich-Khasin-Bushyev, Leningrad 1968 went 12...B-K2 13 R-N1 O-O 14 R×P B×B 15 NK4×B B-N5 16 R×BP QR-B1 17 Q-Q6± — Black had no compensation for the pawn and also had to watch his back rank.

13 Q-B2	O-O
14 Q-N2	

White has ample compensation for the sacrificed pawn. Kamarnitsky-Estrin, Moscow 1945.

B

1 P-K4 P-K4 2 N-KB3 N-QB3 3 P-Q4 P×P 4 B-QB4 N-B3 5 O-O N×P 6 R-K1 P-Q4 7 B×P Q×B 8 N-B3

8 ...	Q-Q1(5)

9 R×N+	B-K2

9...B-K3? is definitely wrong because it does nothing to help Black get his king into safety. Tringov-Rossetto, Amsterdam interzonal 1964 continued 10 N×P N×N 11 R×N Q-B1 12 B-N5 B-Q3 13 N-K4 O-O? (13...P-KR3 is better but 14 Q-R5! still leaves White with a clear plus) 14 N-B6+! and White won.

10 N×P	P-B4

Stronger than the immediate 10...O-O 11 N×N!

11 R-B4	O-O
12 N×N	Q×Q+
13 N×Q	P×N
14 R-B4	B-Q3

This position arose in the game Ragozin-Botvinnik, Leningrad 1930. White should have continued with 15 N-B3 and 16 B-B4 with the better endgame prospects because of Black's weak Q-side pawns.

C

1 P-K4 P-K4 2 N-KB3 N-QB3 3 P-Q4 P×P 4 B-QB4 N-B3 5 O-O N×P 6 R-K1 P-Q4 7 B×P Q×B 8 N-B3

| 8... | Q-QR4(6) |

| 9 N×N | B-K3 |

Not 9...B-K2 10 B-N5 B-K3 11 B×B N×B 12 Q×P± (Keres)

| 10 B-Q2 | |

Black now has four plausible moves at his disposal. We consider:

C1 10...Q-N3
C2 10...B-QN5
C3 10...Q-Q4
C4 10...Q-KB4

C1

1 P-K4 P-K4 2 N-KB3 N-QB3 3 P-Q4 P×P 4 B-QB4 N-B3 5 O-O N×P 6 R-K1 P-Q4 7 B×P Q×B 8 N-B3 Q-QR4 9 N×N B-K3 10 B-Q2

10	...	Q-N3
11	B-N5	P-KR3
12	B-R4	P-KN4

In Tringov-Lilienthal, Sofia 1962, Black tried to relieve the pressure by exchanging bishops. After 12...B-K2 13 B×B K×B however, White had more than one good way to continue, possibly the strongest being Estrin's suggestion 14 N-N3 KR-Q1 15 Q-Q3! with an excellent game for the pawn.

| 13 | N-B6+ | K-Q1 |

Naturally not 13...K-K2?? 14 N-Q5+ wining the Queen.

| 14 | B-N3 | |

White has ample compensation for the sacrificed pawn; Geller-Neishtadt, Leningrad 1956.

C2

1 P-K4 P-K4 2 N-KB5 N-QB3 3 P-Q4 P×P 4 B-QB4 N-B3 5 O-O N×P 6

R-K1 P-Q4 7 B×P Q×B 8 N-B3 Q-QR4 9 N×N B-K3 10 B-Q2

10 ...   B-QN5 (7)

A natural looking move which negates White's threat while simultaneously developing a piece.

11 N×P!   N×N

After 11...B×B 12 N×N P×N 13 Q×B Q×Q 14 N×Q, White has much the better ending because of Black's grotty Q-side pawns.

12 P-QB3

The position has become extremely complicated as a result of White's temporary piece sacrifice. Black has various ways of allowing White to regain the piece, none of which seem to leave his king well placed.

12 ...   B-K2

12...N-K7+?! 13 Q×N B-K2 was tried in Karaklajic-Traikovic, Herzegovina 1949 which continued: 14 Q-Q3! O-O 15 Q-N3 K-R1 16 B-B4 P-QB3 17 B-K5 R-KN1 18 B-Q6!± White's pieces are better placed.
    Black's most serious tries are the two castling moves:
    12...O-O-O 13 P×B Q-KB4?! (13...Q-Q4 is better but 14 B-N5 P-KB3 15 B-B4 still leaves White in command) 14 R-QB1 and now Black is probably unable to stem the tide of White's attack:
    a) 14...B-Q4 15 N-N3 Q-Q2 16 R×P+! K×R 17 B-B4+ K-B1 18 Q×N P-QN3 19 R-K7! with a terrific attack (Analysis by Konstantinopolsky)
    b) 14...K-N1 15 N-N3 Q-N3 16 B-B4 N-N4 17 Q-R4 N-Q3 18 B-K3 P-N3 (or 18...P-QR3 19 Q-R5! R-QB1 20 P-QR4 with a strong attack) 19 R×P! K×R 20 Q×P+ K-B3 21 P-N5+! N×P 22 Q×NP+ K-Q2 23 Q×N+ ±± (Analysis by Estrin) White has a mating attack, e.g. 23...K-K2 24 B-B5+ K-B3 25 Q-N4.
    c) 14...R-Q4 15 N-N3 Q-N3 16 B-B4 N-B3 17 Q-R4 Q-B3 18 B×P K×B 19 P-N5 Q-Q5 20 P-N4 Q-N3 21 P×N R-Q7 22 P×P+ ±± Kinzel-Pfleger, Lenzerheide 1964. Black's king is too exposed.

d) 14...B×P 15 Q-R4! B-Q4 16 N-N3 N-B6+ 17 K-R1! and Black's pieces are left looking ridiculous. Malchev-Gudev, Bulgaria 1960 continued 17...Q-N5 (if 17...Q-Q6 18 B-B4!) 18 P-R3 Q-R5 19 N-B5 Q-B3, and now with Estrin's suggestion 20 R-K7! White's position would have become overwhelming, since 20...Q×N and 20...N×B both allow 21 Q×P forcing mate.

The reader should, by now, be convinced that castling Q-side does not supply Black with the solution to his problems.

12...O-O 13 P×B also seems to be unsavoury for Black. e.g. 13...Q-KB4 14 R-QB1 and now:

a) 14...QR-Q1 15 R-B5 R-Q4 16 N-N3 Fuderer-Djaja, Yugoslav Championship 1948; White wins a piece after 16...Q-Q6 (or 16...Q-N3) 17 R×R B×R 18 B-B3.

b) 14...N-B3 15 R-B5 Q-N5 16 Q×Q B×Q 17 R-KN5 B-K3 18 B-B3! P-B3 19 N×P+ K-B2 20 N-Q5! ±± Van Oosterwijk Bruyn-Van Donk, Soest 1949

c) 14...B×P? 15 R-B5 Q-Q2 (or 15...Q-B1 16 B-B3 N-K3 17 N-B6+! P×N 18 B×P R-Q1 19 Q-N4+ K-B1 20 R-KR5 ±± Matevic-Kalic, Yugoslavia 1956) 16 B-B3 with a very strong attack.

d) 14...P-QN3 (best according to Euwe) 15 B-B3 and White's pieces are better placed; contrast the activity of the rooks!

After 12...O-O 13 P×B, 13...Q-Q4 has been tried in place of 13...Q-KB4. White should still continue with 14 R-QB1 and it is difficult to see how Black has improved on the debacle discussed above—His queen still provides White with a target that can be used to gain a tempo for the attack. e.g.

a) 14...P-QN3 15 R×P QR-Q1 16 B-B3 N-N4 17 Q-B3!± Maric-Gligoric, Sombor 1957 (if now 17...N×R 18 N-B6+! P×N 19 Q×P followed by mate)

b) 14...QR-Q1 15 R-B5 Q×P 16 B-B3 N-N4 (not 16...N-N4? 17 N-B6+! P×N 18 B×P R-Q4 19 Q-Q2! 1-0 Kinzel-Duckstein, Vienna 1958) 17 Q-N4 N-Q5 18 N-B6+ K-R1 19 Q-R4 N-K7+ 20 K-R1 P-KR3 21 R-KR5 and Black cannot prevent himself from being mated, Vitolins-Koriakin, Leningrad 1966.

So castling K-side is also not good enough from Black's point of view. Now back to the main line.

13 P×N   Q-Q4(8)

On 13...Q-KB4 (13...B-QN5? 14 P-Q5!) 14 B-N4 B×B 15 Q-R4+, Black is in greater difficulties than in the main line because his queen is further from the theatre of war. After 15...B-Q2 Trifunovic has shown that 16 N-Q6++! is decisive. e.g.

a) 16...K-B1 17 Q×B.N4 P×N 18 Q×QP+ K-N1 19 R-K5 Q-N5 20 P-KR3 when White regains the piece and the game is over.

b) 16...K-Q1 17 N×NP+ K-B1 18 Q×B.N4 R-QN1 19 N-Q6+ P×N 20 QR-B1+ etc.

Other fifteenth moves are no improvement: 15...P-QN4 16 Q×B P-QR4 17 Q-R3 P-N5 is refuted by 18 Q-R4+ B-Q2 19 N-B5+ when Black's king is kept in the centre.

Finally 15...P-QB3 16 Q×B is clearly overwhelming.

14   R-QB1

Black is given no respite. Now he must attend to the needs of his QBP.

14   ...   P-QB3

Not 14...O-O-O 15 B-B4 P-QB3 16 Q-R4 when White's attack is very strong.

15	B-N5!	B×B
16	R-B5	Q-Q2
17	R×B	O-O-O
18	R×P	Q×P
19	Q×Q	R×Q
20	P-QR3	KR-Q1
21	P-B3	P-KR4
22	P-KR4	

The ending is clearly better for White, because of the vulnerability of Black's KRP and the threat of N-N5. Torman-Vogt, East German Junior Championship 1967.

C3

1 P-K4 P-K4 2 N-KB3 N-QB3 3 P-Q4 P×P 4 B-QB4 N-B3 5 O-O N×P 6 R-K1 P-Q4 7 B×P Q×B 8 N-B3 Q-QR4 9 N×N B-K3 10 B-Q2

10   ...   Q-Q4(*9*)

9

	11 B-N5	B-K2

11...Q-B5 provides White with the convenient regrouping manoeuvre 12 N3-Q2 Q-N4 13 N-QN3. Pogats-Szily, Budapest 1951 continued 13...P-KR3 14 B-R4 Q-N3 15 Q-R5 (threatening 16 N-B6+ P×N 17 R×B+) 15...N-K2 16 N4-B5 when White has some advantage and a very persistent initiative.

11...P-KR3? 12 B-B6! has similar consequences to note (b) to Black's tenth move in variation A.

11...B-Q3 leads to a level ending after 12 B-B6 O-O 13 N×P N×N 14 Q×N Q×Q 15 B×Q KR-Q1.

	12 B×B	K×B

If 12...N×B 13 N×P O-O 14 N×B results in Black's pawns being weakened.

	13 P-B4!	Q×P

If 13...P×Pep 14 Q-B2! is a gambit continuation suggested by Estrin which leads to good attacking chances for White; both Black's king and queen will find life on the open central files very unpleasant.

	14 R-QB1	Q-Q4
	15 R-B5	

The same theme appears again—White's QR enters the fray with gain of tempo on Black's queen.

	15 ...	Q-Q2

Capturing the QRP puts Black's queen offside: 15...Q×P 16 N×P KR-Q1 17 R×N P×R 18 N×P+ K-K1 19 Q-B2! Q-Q4 (if 19...Q-B5? 20 N-Q6+ ±±; or 19...Q-N6 20 N-B6+ K-B1 21 Q×P±±) 20 N×R R×N 21 Q×P± Radulov-Ciocaltea, Bucharest 1961. White's pieces are well co-ordinated and he has the strong threat of 22 N-B5.

	16 Q-B1	QR-QB1
	17 P-QN4!	

With the mortal threat of 18 P-N5 followed by 19 Q-R3.

	17 ...	K-B1

If 17...N×P, 18 N-K5 Q-Q1 19 Q-R3 is still decisive. e.g. 19...P-QN3 20 Q×N! P×R 21 Q×BP+ K-K1 22 N×P±± (Estrin)

	18 P-N5	N-K2
	19 N-K5	Q-Q1
	20 N-N5!	

White has a winning attack. Radulov-Shianovsky, Bulgaria-Ukraine match, Kiev 1962, concluded: 20...P-KR3 21 N.N5-B3 P-KR4 22 N-N5 R-R3 23 Q-KB4 Q-K1 24 N.K5×P! B×N 25 R5-K5 K-N1 26 R×N Q-B1 27 R×B Q-Q3 28 Q-B5 1-0.

C4

1 P-K4 P-K4 2 N-KB3 N-QB3 3 P-Q4 P×P 4 B-QB4 N-B3 5 O-O N×P 6 R-K1 P-Q4 7 B×P Q×B 8 N-B3 Q-QR4 9 N×N B-K3 10 B-Q2.

	10 ...	Q-KB4(*10*)

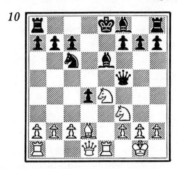

As in many of the similar positions already examined, KB4 is not too good a square for Black's queen.

	11 B-N5	P-KR3

After 11...B-QB4 12 N-R4 Q-Q4, 13 P-QB4! is very strong. 13...P×Pep loses the queen to 14 N-B6+, while 13...Q-K4 (the only other move that keeps the QB defended) is refuted by Estrin's suggestion 14 P-B4! P-Q6+ 15 K-R1 Q-Q5 16 N-KB3. Estrin—Machavariani, Leningrad 1966, continued 16...P-Q7 17 N×Q P×RQ+ 18 Q×Q B×N 19 P-KB5 and White won quickly.

	12 B-R4	B-B4

Not 12...P-KN4?? because of 13 N×QP N×N 14 Q×N P×B 15 N-B6+ K-K2 16 N-Q5+ 1-0, as in Estrin-Riskin, Moscow 1963.

12...Q-Q4? is also a mistake because of 13 B-B6! R-KN1 14 P-B4! Q×P (or 14...Q-Q2 15 Q-N3 B-QN5 16 N-K5! ±) 15 R-QB1 and Black's king will never be able to find a safe haven. Sydor-Dzieciolowski,

Wroclaw 1960.

Now that White's KR4 square is occupied by his bishop he no longer has the possibility 13 N-R4 Q-Q4 14 P-QB4 at his disposal (see previous note).

13	B-N3	O-O
14	N-R4	Q-Q4
15	P-QB4	Q×P
16	R-QB1±	

Pfleger-Neunhoffer, Heidenheim 1959.

White now wins a piece and he has the better game even though Black can gather another pawn or two. Black's Q-side pawns will come under heavy pressure and his king position cannot be considered completely safe.

Part Three: The Max Lange Attack
1 P-K4 P-K4 2 N-KB3 N-QB3 3 P-Q4 P×P 4 B-QB4 (*11*)

11

4	...	N-B3
5	O-O	B-B4

5...B-K2 transposes to an inferior line of the passive Hungarian Defence. One modern example of this outdated debut is the game Zagorovsky-Starovoyt, Mogilev 1966, which continued: 6 P-K5 N-K5 7 B-Q5 P-B4 8 N×P N×N 9 Q×N B-B4 10 Q-B4 Q-K2 11 N-B3! and Black is already in trouble—he will have difficulty completing his development and his king remains stuck in the centre.

5...P-Q4 is also inferior because of 6 P×P N×P 7 R-K1+ B-K3 8 N-N5.

6	P-K5	P-Q4(*12*)

6...N-K5 is a pointless move. It puts the knight on a square from which retreat is, at the moment, impossible, and Black has no dynamic possibilities with which to offset this disadvantage. A game Morphy-Dominguez, Havana 1864, concluded: 7 B-Q5 P-B4 8 P×Pep N×P.B3 9

B-N5 B-K2 10 B×N.KB6 B×B (if 10...P×B 11 N-N5! N-K4 12 Q-R5+N-N3 13 B-B7+K-B1 14 Q-R6 mate) 11 R-K1+ N-K2 12 N-K5 B×N 13 Q-R5+P-KN3 14 Q×B R-B1 15 N-Q2 P-B3 (or 15...P-Q3 16 Q×P.Q4 P-B3 17 B-K6 B×B 18 R×B P-Q4 19 QR-K1 R-B2 20 N-B3±±) 16 N-B4! P-Q3 17 N×P+ K-Q2 18 B-K6+ K-B2 19 N×B+ with mate to follow.

6...N-KN5 is far more sensible, but it would appear that White can get slightly the upper hand with 7 B-B4! and now:

a) 7...O-O? 8 P-KR3! N-R3 9 B×N P×B 10 P-B3 P-Q4 (not 10...P×P 11 N×P P-Q3 12 N-K4! with a very strong attack) 11 B-N3 P×P 12 N×P P-Q5 13 N-Q5! B-K2 (or 13...B-B4 14 Q-B1 B-K2 15 Q×P±) 14 Q-Q3, and Black has no satisfactory defence to the threat of 15 B-B2.

b) 7...P-Q3 8 P×P B×P (Keres refutes 8...P×P with 9 R-K1+ N5-K4 10 B×N! P×B 11 N×KP. If now 11...O-O?? 12 N×P R×N 13 Q-R5±±) 9 R-K1+ K-B1 (not 9...N-K2 10 B×B Q×B 11 Q-K2 when Black cannot castle; nor 9...B-K2 10 B-QN5 O-O 11 B×N P×B 12 N×P± e.g. 12...B-N2 13 N-B5 or 12...B-Q2 13 B×P) 10 B×B+ Q×B 11 P-B3 Q-B4 12 QN-Q2 P-Q6 (12...P×P 13 N-K4!) 13 N-Q4 N×N 14 P×N Q×P 15 Q-B3 Q-B3 16 Q-Q5 'with equality' Keres, but Black still has to survive.

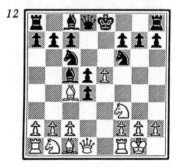

12

7 P×N   P×B
8 R-K1+   B-K3

This is more or less forced, since on 8...K-B1 comes 9 B-N5 P×P (not 9...Q-Q2? 10 B-R6! P×B 11 Q-Q2 when Black resigns) 10 B-R6+ K-N1 11 N-B3! with a tremendous game for the pawn. e.g. 11...B-KN5 12 N-K4 B-KB1 (Kazic-Vukovic, Yugoslavia 1940 went instead 12...P-N3 13 P-B3 N-K4? 14 N×N B×Q 15 N-Q7 B-K2 16 N4×P+ B×N 17 R-K8+! Q×R 18 N×B mate) 13 B×B K×B 14 Q-Q2 K-N2 15 Q-B4 when White's attacking chances against Black's exposed king are enhanced by the possibility of manoeuvring a knight to KB5 or KR5. Or 11...B-B1 12 B×B K×B 13 N-K4 followed by 14 Q-Q2 with a clear advantage to White.

9 N-N5

White's moves each carry a direct threat.

$$9 \dots \qquad\qquad\qquad Q\text{-}Q4(13)$$

Again virtually forced as will be seen from a quick look at the 'alternatives':

a) 9...Q-Q2?? (or 9...Q×P??) 10 N×B P×N 11 Q-R5+ and White wins a piece.

b) 9...Q-Q3 10 N×B P×N 11 P×P R-KN1 12 Q-R5+ K-Q2 13 N-Q2! Q-K2 14 N-K4 B-N5 15 B-N5± Yukhtman-Kim, Tashkent 1950. After 15...Q×P (forced) 16 N-B6+, White's attack should prove too strong.

c) 9...B-QN5 10 P×P R-KN1 11 N×B P×N 12 R×P+ K-B2 13 R-K4 R×P 14 N-Q2 with rich prospects for White (Euwe)

d) 9×P-KN3 10 Q-B3! K-Q2 (or 10...O-O 11 R×B! P×R 12 P-B7+ K-R1 13 N×KP Q-K2 14 B-N5! Q×P 15 N×B± Feilich Veksei, postal game 1920) 11 N×BP! B×N 12 Q-N4+ K-Q3 13 B-B4+ N-K4 14 P-N4! K-B3 15 B×N B×P 16 P-QB3 B-B4 17 P×P White has a won position as Black's king is far too exposed; Estrin-Ginsberg, Moscow 1944.

10	N-QB3	Q-B4
11	N3-K4	

We have now reached a major crossroads in the Max Lange Attack and there are three variations to be examined in detail.

A 11...O-O-O
B 11...B-KB1
C 11...B-N3

11...P×P?? does not come into serious consideration because after 12 P-KN4! Q-K4 13 N-KB3, Black loses his queen.

11...B-Q3 is also bad: 12 N×BP O-O (or 12...K×N 13 N-N5+ and if 13...K-K1 then 14 N×B K-Q2 15 N×NP or if 13...K-N1 14 P×P followed by N×B and N×QP) 13 N7×B P×N 14 P×P K×P 15 Q-Q2±— White has the initiative and Black's pawns are weak.

A

1 P-K4 P-K4 2 N-KB3 N-QB3 3 P-Q4 P×P 4 B-QB4 N-B3 5 O-O B-B4 6 P-K5 P-Q4 7 P×N P×B 8 R-K1+ B-K3 9 N-N5 Q-Q4 10 N-QB3 Q-B4 11 N3-K4

11 ...	O-O-O
12	P-KN4!

At first sight this thrust might appear to be too loosening, but it is the only means by which White can satisfy the dynamic demands of the position. White's returns for the pawn are threefold: (1) Black's QB is vulnerable, being defended only by its queen; (2) Black's queen will be very short of squares for some time to come; and (3) White has the initiative. Only by making good use of these assets can White justify his whole strategy.

When the reader understands this move and appreciates its merits he will not be so surprised to see the move P-KN4 appearing more than once in the course of our examination of the Max Lange.

12 ...	Q-K4

12...Q-Q4 loses the exchange to 13 P×P KR-N1 14 N-B6. The game Chigorin-Albin 1897 continued: 14...Q-Q3 15 N5-K4 Q-K4 16 P-B4 P-Q6+ 17 K-N2 Q-Q5 18 P-B3! and Black's queen was lost.

13	N×B.6	P×N
14	P×P	KR-N1
15	B-R6!	P-Q6!

15...B-N5 looks to be a logical move, removing the bishop from attack with gain of tempo on White's rook and at the same time opening up two new escape squares (QN4 and QR4) for Black's queen. However, Estrin has shown that White's momentum is sufficient for him to be able to force a decisive advantage in reply to 15...B-N5: 16 P-B4! Q-QN4 (if 16...Q-QR4 17 N-B6 B×R 18 Q×B costs Black a tempo because now he must move his queen again since 18...Q×Q+ 19 R×Q P-Q6 20 P×P P×P 21 N×R R×N 22 R-Q1 wins easily for White) 17 N-B6 B×R (in reply to 17...Q-QB4 White has the simple move 18 K-N2 at his disposal, while 17...P-Q6 is met by 18 N×R) 18 Q×B P-K4 19 N×R R×N 20 P-B5 and White's passed pawns give him a winning position as in Estrin-Chuckov, Moscow 1940.

15...B-K2 16 Q-B3 P-Q6 17 P-B3 transposes to the text.

16	P-QB3	B-K2(*14*)

In Marshall-Tarrasch, Hamburg 1910, Q3 was shown to be the wrong square for the bishop: 16...B-Q3 17 P-B4 Q-Q4 18 Q-B3 B-K2 19 P-N5 Q-KB4 20 N-N3 Q-B2 21 Q-N4 QR-K1? 22 R-K4! P-N4 (if 22...N-R4 23 QR-K1 K-Q2 24 P-B5±±) 23 P-QR4! and Black's position was falling apart. The game concluded: 23...P-R3 24 P×P P×P 25 K-N2! N-Q1 (if 25...B-Q3 26 N-R5±±) 26 Q-B3 Q-N3 27 R-Q4! P-B3 28 R×N+ K×R 29 Q×BP 1-0

From similar vintage comes a more active try in 16...P-Q7. This move was played with success against Marshall by Leonhardt in 1911. White's best line seems to be 17 R-K2 R-Q6 18 N×B Q×N 19 R×QP N-K4 20 R×R P×R 21 K-N2! Q-Q4+ 22 K-N3. The game Radulov-Sokolov, Sofia-Belgrade match 1961, continued 22...N-B2 23 Q-Q2 Q-K5 (23...Q-Q3+ 24 K-N2 P-K4 25 P-N5 N-Q1, with chances for both sides, is better) and now 24 R-K1! is quite strong (±)24...Q-N3 25 B-B4 R×P 26 P-KR3 P-KR4 27 P-B3, with the threat of 28 Q-K3 attacking the KP and QRP.

14

17	P-B4	Q-Q4
18	Q-Q2	

White's last two moves initiate a plan suggested by Sokolsky whereby White threatens to double rooks on the K-file and follows this up with N-B2.

18 	 ... 	 R-Q2

In a 1949 USSR correspondence game, Kochergin-Homsky, Black tried to manoeuvre 18...N-N1?! 19 R-K3 N-Q2. Play continued 20 P-N5 Q-KB4 21 R-KB1 N-B4 22 N-N3 Q-N5, and now with 23 K-N2! followed by 24 P-KR3, White could have maintained a clear plus.

18...B-B4+ 19 N×B Q×N+ 20 Q-K3 Q×Q+ 21 R×Q leaves White with virtually a winning position. One of his K-side pawns will surely promote.

19 	 R-K3 	 N-Q1

Heading for KB2.

20	P-N3	N-B2·
21	P×P	Q-QR4
.

22	R-R3	N×B
23	R×N	R×P
24	P-N5	Q-KB4

This complicated position presents difficulties to both sides. Markelov-Ostroverkhov, corres 1951-52.

B

1 P-K4 P-K4 2 N-KB3 N-QB3 3 P-Q4 P×P 4 B-QB4 N-B3 5 O-O B-B4 6 P-K5 P-Q4 7 P×N P×B 8 R-K1+ B-K3 9 N-N5 Q-Q4 10 N-QB3 Q-B4 11 N3-K4

	11	...	B-KB1(*15*)

Rubinstein's move, leading to a terrible position for Black.

| | 12 | N×BP | K×N |

Naturally not 12...B×N?? 13 N-Q6++ end of game.

| | 13 | N-N5+ | K-N1 |

13...K-N3, as might be expected, is far too risky: After 14 N×B P×P 15 P-KN4! (that move again) 15...Q-QR4 16 B-B4, White's forces are well co-ordinated and Black's king is somewhat unsafe. The 1949 correspondence game Crowl-Kloss concluded: 16...B-Q3 17 B×B P×B 18 P-N4! N×P 19 Q×P P-Q4 20 Q-B4 QR-KN1 21 Q-B5+ K-B2 22 P-N5 R-N3 23 P-KR4 KR-KN1 24 K-R1 1-O (White was threatening both 25 P×P followed by 26 N-N5+ and 25 N-B4 R3-N2 26 Q-Q7+ [or 26 Q-K6+] and mate.)

| | 14 | P-KN4! |

Here it is again!

| | 14 | ... | Q-N3 |

All other moves lose at once, e.g.:

a) 14...Q×P.B3 15 R×B Q-Q1 16 Q-B3 Q-Q2 17 R-K7!! 1-0 Sämisch-Raiman, Bremen 1929;

b) 14...Q-Q4 15 N×B N-K4? 16 P-B7+! K×P 17 N-N5+ K-N1 18 R×N! Q×R 19 Q-B3 1-0 Denker-Avram, New York 1944 and Sazhakv-

Romanishin, Lvov 1947;

c) 14...Q×NP+?? 15 Q×Q B×Q 16 P-B7 mate.

15	R×B	P×P
15	Q-B3	K-N2

If 16...N-K4 17 R×N! P×R 18 Q-Q5+ K-N2 19 N-K6+ K-N1 20 N-Q8+! K-N2 21 Q×KP+; or 16...B-K2 17 P-KR4 N-K4 18 R×N! P×R 19 Q-Q5+ followed by N-K6+. White's attack wins quickly in each case.

17	B-B4!	N-Q1

If Black defends his QBP by 17...B-Q3, he allows White an extra tempo for the attack. Estrin now analyses 18 P-KR4 B×B 19 Q×B KR-K1 20 Q×QBP+ K-N1 21 QR-K1 R×R 22 R×R Q-N2 23 R×N P×R 24 Q×BP R-N1 25 Q×QBP+ K-R1 26 N-B7+ K-N1 27 N-Q6+ K-R1 28 Q×P. White has three pawns for the exchange and should experience little difficulty in converting this advantage into a win. e.g. 28...R×P 29 N-B7+ (29 Q×R?? allows perpetual check) 29...K-N1 30 N-R6+ Q×N 31 Q×R Q×P 32 Q-N8+ and the ending is an easy win.

18	R-K4	P-KR4

If 18...P-QB4, 19 QR-K1 adds fuel to the attack.

19	R×P	P×P
20	R-Q7+	N-B2
21	Q×KNP	P×N
22	B-K5+±±	

Estrin-Webitsky, Moscow 1939. White should win comfortably; Black's king is unsafe and White can readily regain his sacrificed material.

C

1 P-K4 P-K4 2 N-KB3 N-QB3 3 P-Q4 P×P 4 B-QB4 N-B3 5 O-O B-B4 6 P-K5 P-Q4 7 P×N P×B 8 R-K1+ B-K3 9 N-N5 Q-Q4 10 N-QB3 Q-B4 11 N3-K4

11	...	B-N3(*16*)

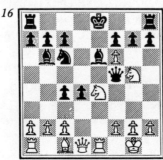

16

	12	P×P	R-KN1
	13	P-KN4!	

What else!

	13	...	Q-N3
	14	N×B	P×N
	15	B-N5!	

The first move of a new wave of attack that guarantees White a clear advantage.

15   ...   R×P

15...P-KR3 fails to 16 Q-B3! and if 16...P×B then White wins by force: 17 N-B6+ K-B2 18 R×P K×R 19 R-K1+ N-K4 20 Q-Q5+ K×N 21 Q×N+ followed by mate, or if 16...R×P then 17 N-B6+ with a similar win.

15...P-Q6 accomplishes nothing after 16 P×P! e.g. 16...P×P 17 Q×P R×P 18 QR-Q1 R-B2 19 P-KR4± (correspondence game Abezs and Kosmann—Zemsch and Chigorin)—White has an easy attack against Black's stranded king, or 16...R×P 17 P×P B-Q5 18 P-KR3 R-B2 19 K-N2 followed by P-B4 (±) as in another correspondence game between the same opponents.

16   Q-B3!

Threatening 17 N-B6+ followed by 18 R×P.

16   ...   K-Q2

Other defensive moves have been tried here without success.

a) 16...P-K4 17 N-B6+ K-B2 (or 17...K-K2 18 P-KR4 R-B2 19 R×P+ N×R 20 R-K1 K-B1 21 R×N±±) 18 P-KR4! P-KR3 19 N-K4+ K-K3 20 P-R5 Q-B2 21 B-B6 R2-N1 22 Q-B5+ K-Q4 23 P-N3 R×P+ 24 Q×R R-KN1 25 P×P+ K×P 26 B-N5 P×B 27 Q-N3 1-0 Chigorin-Teichmann, London 1899; once again Black's king proves to be too exposed in these lines.

b) 16...R-B2 17 N-B6+ R×N 18 Q×R Q×Q 19 B×Q K-B2 20 P-N5 and White's material advantage should prove decisive;

c) 16...P-KR3 17 N-B6+ K-Q1 18 R×P N-K2 19 B×P! Q×B 20 Q-Q5+ and Black is being mated. Holzhausen-Zoege, Leipzig 1899.

	17	N-B6+	K-B1
	18	R×P!	Q×B

Or 18...N-Q1 19 R-K5±±

19   P-KR4!(*17*)

Zemsch now analyses:

a) 19...Q×RP?? 20 R-K8+ N-Q1 21 Q-B5+ followed by mate

b) 19...Q-N3 20 P-R5 Q-N4 (if 20...Q×BP then 21 Q-Q5±±) 21 QR-K1 N-Q1 22 R6-K5 Q-R5 23 R-K8 P-B3 24 Q-B5+ K-N1 25 P-R6! Q×RP (or 25...R-B2 26 Q-K5+ wins the rook with a couple of checks.) 26 Q-K5+ K-B1 27 Q-K6+ and White will give a knight check discovering an attack on Black's queen.

c) 19...Q-QR4 20 R-K8+ N-Q1 21 N-Q5 P-B3 (on 21...R-Q2 22 Q-B5 Q×N White mates by 23 R×N+ etc.) 22 Q-B5+ R-Q2 23 N-K7+ K-B2 24 Q-B4+ R-Q3 25 N-B5±±

d) 19...Q-N4 20 P-QR4 Q-QB4 21 QR-K1 N-Q1 22 R-K8 P-B3 23 R1-K5 Q-Q3 24 Q-B5+ K-N1 25 R5-K6 Q-N5 26 Q-B4+ K-B1 27 N-K4 B-B2 (or 27...P-QR3 28 N-Q6+ K-N1 29 N-B7+ K-R2 30 N×N±±) 28 Q-B5 K-N1 29 R×N+! with a winning attack. e.g. 29...B×R 30 Q-K5+ R-QB2 31 R-K8 P-QR4 32 R×B+ K-R2 33 Q×QP+ P-N3 34 R×R+ K×R 35 Q-Q8+ K-N2 36 N-Q6+ K-R3 37 Q-R8+ and mate in two.

This last variation is an excellent illustration of the vulnerability of Black's king when on the Q-side and of the poor co-ordination of Black's pieces.

2 Petroff's Defence

1 P-K4 P-K4 2 N-KB3 N-KB3

This defence, often quite rightly so, has the reputation of being dull, solid and marginally inferior for Black. It usually leads to symmetrical or nearly-symmetrical positions in which White's advantage may only lie in his one move initiative, and it is this very initiative which White must exploit if he is to emerge with a tangible plus. Of White's major alternatives at move three, we examine the variations commencing with:

3 P-Q4 (*18*)

Black must now decide whether he wishes to fight in an open position or if he prefers to maintain the closed and symmetrical nature of the defence.

We therefore examine:

A 3...P×P

B 3...N×P

Other moves do not warrant a serious study. 3...P-Q3 merely transposes to Philidor's Defence (page XX). 3...P-Q4?! was tried in the game Stein-Bronstein, USSR Championship 1966-7. After 4 KP×P P×P (if 4...P-K5 5 N-K5 N×P 6 B-QB4 B-K3 7 O-O+ — Black's advanced KP will become a target.) 5 B-QN5+ P-B3 (or 5...B-Q2 6 N×P N×P 7 O-O±) 6 P×P P×P 7 B-K2! B-QB4 8 P-B3 P×P 9 Q×Q+ K×Q 10 N×P K-K2 11 O-O R-Q1, White could have increased his advantage with

Stein's post mortem suggestion 12 N-QR4! e.g. 12...B-N3 13 P-QN3! B-B2 14 B-K3! or 12...B-Q3 13 B-K3! N-Q4 14 B-Q4 P-B3 15 KR-B1 and in each case Black's isolated QBP gives him the inferior game.

A

1 P-K4 P-K4 2 N-KB3 N-KB3 3 P-Q4

3 ...	P×P
4 P-K5	N-K5
5 Q×P	P-Q4
6 P×Pep	N×QP
7 B-Q3(*19*)	

The game has taken on an open character. White's pieces have no development problems and the apparently exposed position of his queen cannot be exploited to any real extent.

7 ...	N-B3

The most natural move, developing a piece with gain of tempo. Another idea which has been tried in this position is Bronstein's 7...Q-K2+ 8 B-K3 which merely helps White's development. e.g.

a) 8...B-B4 9 N-B3 N-B3 10 Q-QR4 B×B 11 P×B Q-Q2 12 P-Q4 B-K2 13 P-Q5 N-N1 14 Q-N3± Bronstein-Holmov USSR Championship 1959; White's advanced QP gives him a useful space advantage.

b) 8...N-B4 9 B×N B×B 10 N-B3 with a big lead in development (Keres);

c) 8...N-B3 9 Q-KB4 P-KN3 10 N-B3 B-K3 (or 10...B-N2 11 N-Q5 Q-Q1 12 O-O-O O-O, when White can launch a dangerous attack with 13 P-KR4!) 11 N-Q4 B-N2 12 N×N P×N 13 O-O O-O-O 14 B-Q4± (Black has pawn weaknesses) Spassky-Rossetto, Amsterdam interzonal, 1964.

8 Q-KB4	P-KN3

Again the most natural. 8...Q-K2+ 9 B-K3 transposes to variation (b) in the above note. 8...B-K2 is a less sensible plan than the text because not only does Black wish to develop his KB but he should also concern himself with the safety of his K-side.

After 9 N-B3 B-K3 10 B-Q2! Q-Q2 11 O-O-O, Black hardly dares castle K-side (11...O-O? 12 P-KR4! P-KR3 13 N-KN5!! with a terrific attack) while 11...O-O-O is also not without its drawbacks: 12 KR-K1 P-KR3 13 B-K3± Suetin-Pollack, 1958.

8...B-K3 was another try employed by Rossetto in the 1964 interzonal, this one meeting with a similar lack of success to that used in this game with Spassky (see note c to Black's seventh move). Evans-Rossetto continued 9 B-Q2 Q-Q2 (9...P-KN3? 10 B-B3) 10 O-O O-O-O 11 N-B3 P-KR3 (11...B-K2 is a little better though White still retains a plus after 12 Q-QR4 K-N1 13 B-K3) 12 Q-QR4 K-N1 13 B-K3± (White is threatening 14 N-K5).

9 O-O	B-N2
10 B-Q2!(*20*)	

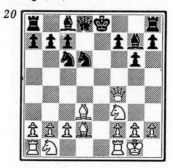

A very interesting yet rarely played move. White offers the exchange and a pawn and in return for acceptance of any of all of this material he receives ample compensation in the removal from the board of Black's KB. The resulting position is one from which Black experiences great problems of survival, so detrimental are the dark square weaknesses near his king.

If Black declines the proffered gifts his problems are still not solved; White continues with B-QB3 and has pressure along the long diagonal towards the enemy king.

10 ...	O-O

Let us examine the sort of fate that can befall Black if he grabs the pawn (10...BxP?! 11 B-B3):

a) 11...BxR 12 BxB O-O (or 12...R-KN1 13 B-B6±) 13 B-B6 and White has a terrific attack. e.g. 13...Q-Q2 14 Q-R6 N-K1 15 B-N7! NxB 16 N-N5 winning;

b) 11...BxB 12 NxB B-K3 (if 12...O-O then 13 N-Q5!) 13 KR-K1 O-O 14 N-KN5 N-K1 15 Q-KR4 N-B3 16 Q-R6! B-Q4 (so far we have been following the 1958 correspondence game Neumann-Spala) 17 QR-Q1, and White's attack provides superfluous compensation for the pawn.

10...Q-B3 is a move suggested by Mikenas with the idea of relieving the pressure by forcing the exchange of queens. After 11 Q×Q B×Q 12 N-B3 B-K3 13 N-KN5, however, White's initiative and the exposed position of Black's king combine to give the first player a slight plus.

11	B-B3	B-B4

11...P-B3 was tried in Levy-Balshan, Haifa 1970, and after 12 QN-Q2 N-K2, White could have maintained his pressure against Black's K-side with 13 Q-Q4!

12	R-Q1	Q-K2
13	B.B3×B	K×B

Now White's strategy has been fulfilled — Black's fianchettoed bishop has been exchanged bringing about the consequential weakening of his K-side.

14	N-B3	B-K3
15	B-N5!	N-Q1
16	N-N5	P-KB3
17	N5-K4	

Matsukevich-Chesnauskas, Leningrad 1964. White has strong pressure against Black's position.

B

1 P-K4 P-K4 2 N-KB3 N-KB3 3 P-Q4

3 ...	N×P

This move leads to a more closed type of position than 3...P×P.

4	B-Q3	P-Q4
5	N×P(*21*)	

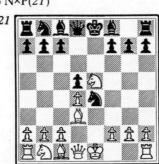

There is one relevant observation which is worth mentioning at this point. One of the other main lines of Petroff's Defence runs: 1 P-K4 P-

K4 2 N-KB3 N-KB3 3 N×P P-Q3 4 N-KB3 N×P 5 P-Q4 thus arriving at
a position with identical pawn structure to that in the above diagram.
The difference between the two positions is that in the column White
seems to have played both B-Q3 and N-K5 at the same time as
compared with the other line. Thus, within the first five moves, White
has, in effect, gained a tempo over another main line.

Black now has three plausible possibilities.

B1 5...B-K2
B2 5...N-Q2
B3 5...B-Q3

5...P-QB4 may be strongly met by either 6 Q-K2(±) or 6 B-
QN5+(±). If 5...N-QB3 6 N×N P×N 7 P-QB4 e.g. 7...Q-K2 8 O-O P-
KN3 9 B×N Q×B (or 9...P×B 10 R-K1 P-KB4 11 P-B3±) 10 Q-Q2!±.

If 5...B-K3 6 Q-K2! N-Q3 7 O-O B-K2 8 N-Q2 O-O 9 R-K1 B-B4 10
N-N3 B×B 11 Q×B N-Q2 12 N-B5± Minic-Rogoff, Zagreb 1971

B1
1 P-K4 P-K4 2 N-KB3 N-KB3 3 P-Q4 N×P 4 B-Q3 P-Q4 5 N×P

	5 ...	B-K2
	6 O-O	O-O

On 6...N-Q2, 7 B-KB4 is strong. e.g. 7...N×N 8 B4×N O-O 9 P-QB4
P-QB3 10 Q-B2± Black must play 10...P-KB4, giving White un-
disturbed use of his K5 square while the black knight can be driven
away at any time by P-KB3.

	7 P-QB4	N-KB3

If 7...P-QB3 8 P×P P×P 9 B×N P×B 10 N-QB3 and White wins a
pawn: 10...B-KB4 11 R-K1 N-Q2 12 B-B4! N-B3 13 B-N5!

	8 N-QB3	QN-Q2

8...B-K3 9 P-B5! was shown to be very good for White as early as
1913.

8...P×P 9 B×BP N-B3 gives White a free hand in the centre: 10 B-K3
B-Q3 11 P-B4 N-K2 12 Q-N3! (Euwe); Black has a terrible position,
e.g. 12...Q-K1 13 QR-K1.

9	B-N5	P×P
10	B×BP	N-N3
11	B-N3	N.B3-Q4
12	B×B	N×B
13	Q-B3!±	

White has the more fluid position. Gligoric-Gudmundsson,
Amsterdam 1950, continued: 13...B-K3 14 B×B P×B 15 Q×P Q×P 16

Q×BP N2-Q4 17 Q-Q6 and White is a safe pawn up.

B 2

1 P-K4 P-K4 2 N-KB3 N-KB3 3 P-Q4 N×P 4 B-Q3 P-Q4 5 N×P

<pre>
        5 ...   N-Q2(22)
</pre>

22

<pre>
        6 Q-K2   N×N
</pre>

6...Q-K2 puts the queen on a square from which her tactical usefulness is heavily outweighed by various other factors: 7 B×N P×B 8 B-B4 N×N 9 B×N P-KB3 10 B-N3 P-KB4 11 N-B3 P-B3 12 O-O-O Q-N4+ (12...B-K3 13 P-Q5!) 13 K-N1 B-N5 14 N-N5! and Black is lost. Dely-Malich, Pecs 1964, concluded: 14...P-B5 15 N-B7+ K-B1 16 Q×P 1-0.

<pre>
        7 B×N   P×B
</pre>

7...Q-R5 fails to 8 B-B3 Q×QP 9 P-B3 winning a piece.

<pre>
        8   Q×P   B-K3
        9   P×N   B-Q4
        10 Q-KN4   P-KR4
        11 Q-R3   Q-K2
        12 P-KB4   P-KN4
</pre>

According to Igor Zaitsev Black has sufficient counterplay, but Euwe points out that 13 N-B3 B-B3 14 B-Q2! maintains White's plus. e.g. 14...P×P 15 O-O-O R-KN1 16 Q×P B×NP 17 KR-K1± or 14...P-N5 15 Q-N3 P-R5 16 Q×NP P-R6 17 O-O-O P×P 18 KR-K1 R×P 19 N-K4±

B3

1 P-K4 P-K4 2 N-KB3 N-KB3 3 P-Q4 N×P 4 B-Q3 P-Q4 5 N×P

<pre>
        5 ...   B-Q3(23)
</pre>

The usual move, and one which we shall attempt to discredit by means of an idea which originated in the last century.

<pre>
        6 N-QB3!   N-KB3
</pre>

6...N×N 7 P×N is a continuation that was seen as early as Barry-

23

Showalter, 1896, but for the purpose of our discussion we shall consider only games that are devoid of cobwebs. Smyslov-Lilienthal, USSR 1941, continued 7...Q-R5 8 O-O O-O 9 R-K1 N-Q2 10 P-KN3 Q-R6 11 B-B1 and White has the edge because he can continue to harass Black's queen.

After 6...B-QN5 White can safely castle, since after 7 O-O N×N 8 P×N B×P 9 B-R3, Black cannot castle K-side and the exchange is taboo because of 9...B×R 10 Q-R5 P-KN3 11 N×NP±± 7...B×N 8 P×B N×QBP would also be bad on account of 9 Q-R5 when Black's king is again under pressure and his knight is stuck out on a rather useless limb.

7	O-O	N-B3	
8	R-K1	O-O	
9	B-KN5		

Threatening both 10 N×QP and 10 B×N followed by 11 N×QP.

9	...	B-K3

Not 9...N×P? 10 B×P+ K×B 11 Q×N, when Black's king's position has been weakened.

10	N-N5	B-K2
11	B-KB4	

Threatening 12 N×N followed by 13 N×BP.

11	...	N×N

Since 11...N-K1 allows 12 Q-R5 and if 12...P-KN3 then 13 N×NP and Black's roof caves in.

12	P×N	N-Q2
13	P-QB3	R-K1
14	N-Q4	N-B1
15	Q-R5	

White has a very dangerous attack against the Black king. Gligoric-Alexander, Dublin zonal tournament 1957, concluded: 15...P-KN3 16

Q-R6 Q-Q2 17 B-KN5 (threatening 18 B-B6 followed by mate) 17...BxB 18 QxB Q-K2 19 Q-N3 B-Q2 (19...P-QB4 allows 20 N-N5 followed by N-Q6.) 20 P-KB4 P-QB4 21 N-B3 P-B4 (to prevent 22 P-B5) 22 в-в2 K-R1 (not 22...N-K3 23 BxP±±) 23 QR-Q1 B-B3 24 N-N5 N-K3 25 NxN QxN 26 R-Q2 P-QR4 27 B-Q1 QR-Q1 28 B-B3 R-Q2 29 Q-B2 P-N3 30 P-KR3 R1-Q1 31 Q-R4! (theatening 32 Q-B6+ QxQ 33 PxC followed by R-K6) 31...R-KB1 (31...Q-K2 32 Q-B6+±±; 31...P-Q5? 32 BxB QxB 33 P-K6 R-Q3 34 Q-B6+ K-N1 35 Q-B7+ K-R1 36 P-K7) 32 K-R2 R-KN2 33 Q-N5 R-Q2 34 R1-Q1 K-N2 35 Q-R4 P-R4 36 Q-N5 K-R2 37 R-K1 R-K1 38 P-KN4 RPxP 39 PxP K-N1 40 K-N3 R-KR2 41 P-B4 BPxP 42 BxNP 1-0. (The analysis has been taken from Gligoric's notes in *Chess.*)

3 Philidor's Defence

1 P-K4 P-K4 2 N-KB3 P-Q3

This defence, in common with the Centre Counter, Nimzoitwsch's Defence and the Greco Counter Gambit, is almost obsolete in top rank chess because experience shows it to be lacking. Black's intention is to play a slow, somewhat cramped defensive game, eventually breaking out with the queen's side thrust . . .P-QN4.

Out suggested counter to Philidor's Defence often produces the open type of position in which the tactical player should revel. In addition, it leaves White (in the main line) with a distinct plus which with due care and attention ought to be convertible into the full point.

3 P-Q4(24)

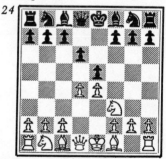

At once staking a firm claim in the centre.

3 ...   N-Q2

Known as the Hanham Variation, this line is usually considered stronger than any of the alternatives:

a) 3...P-KB4? 4 B-QB4! BP×P (or 4...KP×P 5 N-N5! N-KR3 6 N×P R×N 7 Q-R5+ K-Q2 8 Q-N6 R-R1 9 B×N R×B 10 Q×BP+ followed by mate) 5 N×P! P-Q4 (on 5...P×N comes 6 Q-R5+ K-Q2 7 Q-B5+ K-B3 8 Q×P.K5 P-QR3 9 P-Q5+ K-N3 10 B-K3+ etc.) 6 Q-R5+ P-KN3 7 N×P N-KB3 8 Q-K5+ B-K2 9 Q×B+ Q×Q 10 N×Q K×N 11 B-K2 R-N1 12 P-KN3. In compensation for being only a pawn ahead, White has the better position.

b) 3...N-KB3 4 N-B3 QN-Q2 (4...P×P 5 Q×P will transpose to note (d)) 5 B-QB4 B-K2 6 P×P! P×P? allows the combination 7 N-KN5! O-O 8 B×P+ R×B 9 N-K6 Q-K1 10 N×BP Q-Q1 11 N×R. Black must now make an immediate attempt to trap White's seemingly stranded knight, but it appears that the first player has a simple resource which enables him to retain a winning material advantage: 11...P-QN4 12 N-Q5! N×N (if 12...N×P 13 O-O B-B4 14 B-K3 etc.) 13 Q×N N-B3 14 Q×NP B-KN5 15 O-O Q×N 16 P-QB3 B-Q2 17 Q×P. With rook and three pawns for two minor pieces White's material advantage should prove decisive. Magergut-Freidin, Moscow 1955.

c) 3...B-N5? 4 P×P B×N 5 Q×B P×P 6 B-QB4 Q-Q2 7 Q-QN3± (Keres)

d) 3...P×P 4 Q×P! N-QB3 (if 4...B-Q2 5 B-KB4 N-QB3 6 Q-Q2 N-B3 7 N-B3 B-K2 8 O-O-O, or 4...N-KB3 5 B-KN5 B-K2 6 N-B3 O-O 7 O-O-O N-B3 8 Q-Q2, in each case with the freer game and better attacking prospects for White. Analysis by Keres.) 5 B-QN5 B-Q2 6 B×N B×B 7 N-B3 N-B3 8 B-N5 B-K2 9 O-O-O O-O 10 KR-K1! Again White's game is the more fluid and his attacking chances somewhat better than Black's. Lasker-Speyer, 1909.

4 B-QB4	P-QB3

This is one of the key moves in Black's system. Eventually it is intended to support the advance . . P-QN4. In fact, there is no reasonable alternative: e.g.

a) 4...B-K2 5 P×P N×P (not 5...P×P 6 Q-Q5! end of game.) 6 N×N P×N 7 Q-R5 and White wins a pawn.

b) 4...P-KR3? 5 P×P P×P (or 5...N×P 6 N×N P×N 7 B×P+ etc.) 6 B×P+! K×B 7 N×P+ K-B3 8 Q-Q4 with a killing attack. Rohachek-Stulik, Karlovy Vary 1948.

c) 4...KN-B3 5 P×P N×P (5...P×P 6 N-N5!) 6 N×N P×N 7 B×P+ K×B 8 Q×Q B-QN5+ 9 Q-Q2 B×Q+ 10 N×Q and White has won a pawn.

5 N-B3!	

This simple developing move leaves Black with no satisfactory reply.

5 ...	B-K2

The most usual move. If 5...P-KR3 6 P-QR4! and Black's Q-side play has been restricted. Play might continue 6...B-K2 7 O-O KN-B3 8 P-QN3! Q-B2 9 B-N2, and now 9...O-O 10 Q-Q2 is clearly better for White, while 9...N-B1 is refuted by 10 P×P P×P 11 N×P! Q×N 12 N-Q5 Q-Q3 13 B-R3 P-B4 14 P-K5 as in Nimzowitsch-Marco, Gothenburg 1920. Naturally not 5...KN-B3? 6 N-KN5.

6 P×P!	P×P

After 6...N×P Black loses a pawn to 7 N×N P×N 8 Q-R5.

                        7 N-KN5   B×N

7...N-R3 is also bad for Black, the refutation coming as a consequence of his congested central pieces: 8 N-K6! P×N 9 B×N N-N3 (9...P×B 10 Q-R5+ K-B1 11 B×P is followed by mate) 10 Q-R5+ K-B1 (10...P-N3 11 Q-K2 wins) 11 B-N3! P×B 12 R-Q1 Q-K1 (or 12...Q-B2 13 Q×RP+ K-N1 14 R-Q3 B-B1 15 B×P+ B×B 16 Q×B.K6+ Q-B2 17 R-N3+ B-N2 18 Q×KP, when White has three pawns for the piece and his attack is still dangerous. Analysis by Euwe.) 13 Q×RP+ K-B2 (13...K-N1 is also answered by 14 R-Q3!) 14 R-Q3 B-B3 15 R-B3 N-Q2 (or 15...Q-Q1 16 P-N4) 16 P-N4. This position arose in the game Matulovic-Tomovic, Yugoslav Championship 1957, in which White experienced little difficulty in smashing Black's remaining defences: 16...K-N1 17 P-N5 K-B2 18 P×B 1-0.

                        8 Q-R5   P-KN3

Or 8...Q-B3 9 B×B Q-N3 10 Q-R4± Schlechter-Alekhine, Hamburg 1910.

                        9 Q×B   Q×Q
                        10 B×Q(*25*)

25

This semi-ending has been reached more than once in master chess and there is universal agreement that it offers White almost certain victory. Barden-Klein, British Championship 1950, continued: 10...N-B1 11 O-O-O B-K3 12 B-K2 P-B3 (or 12...N-Q2 13 R-Q6 N-K2 14 KR-Q1 P-KR3 15 B-K3 R-Q1 16 P-B4 when White has a strong initiative, Tal-Menvielle, Palma de Mallorca 1966) 13 B-K3 N-K2 14 R-Q2 N-B1 15 KR-Q1 N-N3 16 R-Q6 P-KR4 17 P-QR4 N.N3-Q2. Now, with 18 P-QN4 followed by P-N5, White forces the entry of his knight or the win of Black's QBP. In either case Black's position collapses.

4 Latvian (Greco-Counter) Gambit

1 P-K4 P-K4 2 N-KB3 P-KB4

This ultra sharp reaction by Black produces the sort of game that should really only be seen in a 5-minute competition though the author must confess to having lost against the gambit in a world student championship some years ago. If White puts a foot wrong he can easily find himself being battered to a premature death, but by sticking to a straight and narrow path constructed by Keres, he can be certain of turning the mêlée to his advantage and emerging with a winning position.

3 B-B4(*26*)

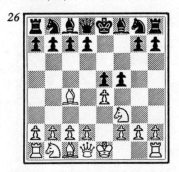

26

The start of a long, forcing sequence in the course of which White sacrifices most of his pieces.

3 ...   P×P

3...P-Q3 transposed to Philidor's Defence (see page XX) while 3...N-KB3 4 N×P Q-K2 5 P-Q4 P-Q3 6 N-B7 seems to be quite good for White.

4 N×P   Q-N4

If 4...P-Q4 5 Q-R5+ P-KN3 6 N×P N-KB3 7 Q-K5+ B-K2 8 B-N5+ P-B3 (or 8...B-Q2 9 B×B+ QN×B 10 Q×B+ Q×Q 11 N×Q K×N 12 P-Q4 and White's extra pawn will be decisive) 9 N×B Q×N 10 Q×Q+ K×Q 11 B-K2 R-KN1 12 P-KN3, and White has a won game.

5 P-Q4!	Q×P
6 Q-R5+	P-KN3

6...K-Q1 allows a quick mate by 7 N-B7+ K-K1 8 N-Q6++ K-K2 9 Q-K5+ etc.

7 B-B7+	K-Q1

If 7...K-K2 8 B-N5+ N-KB3 (8...K-Q3 9 N-B4+ K-B3 10 N-QB3! is no better for Black.) 9 Q-R4 Q×R+ 10 K-Q2 B-N2 11 N-B3 Q×R 12 B×N+ B×B 13 N-Q5+ with a quick win.

8 B×P	Q×R+

Thematic! Keres' analysis refutes all the alternatives with a bluntness equal only to that of the text:

a) 8...B-N5+ 9 K-K2 Q×R 10 B-N5+ B-K2 11 N-B7+ K-K1 12 N×R+ K-Q1 13 N-B7+ K-K1 14 N-K5+ K-Q1 15 Q×P and White wins a piece or two.

b) 8...P-Q3 9 Q-N5+ Q×Q 10 B×Q+ B-K2 11 B×B+ and White nets the exchange with N-B7.

c) 8...P×B 9 B-N5+ B-K2 10 Q×R±±2

d) 8...N-KB3 9 N-B7+ K-K1 10 N×R+ P×B (or 10...K-Q1 11 B-N5±±) 11 Q×P+ leaves White comfortably ahead on material.

9 K-K2(27)

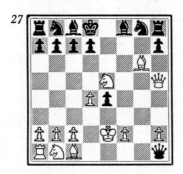

Black now has three plausible possibilities:

A 9...P-Q3
B 9...P-B3 (!)
C 9...Q×B

9...P×B loses quickly to 10 B-N5+ B-K2 11 Q×R B×B 12 Q×N+ K-K2 13 Q-B7+ K-Q3 14 N-QB3! and mating (N-N5) or winning the queen, and 9...Q-N7 to 10 N-B7+ K-K1 11 N-Q6++ K-Q1 12 B×KP N-KB3 13 B-N5±±.

A

1 P-K4 P-K4 2 N-KB3 P-KB4 3 B-B4 P×P 4 N×P Q-N4 5 P-Q4! Q×P
6 Q-R5+ P-KN3 7 B-B7+ K-Q1 8 B×P Q×R+ 9 K-K2

9...		P-Q3
10	N-QB3!	

Threatening 11 B-N5+ winning the queen.

10	...	B-K2

If 10...N-K2 11 N-B7+ wins. e.g. 11...K-Q2 12 B×KP Q-N8 13 B-
B5+ N×B 14 Q×N+ K-K1 15 Q×B+ K×N 16 Q-B5+ or 11...K-K1 12
N×QP++ followed by 13 B×KP.

11	N-B7+	K-K1
12	N×QP++	K-Q1

If 12...K-Q2 13 Q-KB5+ ±± or 12...K-B1 13 B-R6+ ±±

13	N-B7+	K-K1
14	N×R+	P×B

Or 14...K-Q1 15 Q-Q5+

15	Q×P+	K-Q2
16	Q-B5+	K-Q1
17	Q-Q5+	B-Q2

17...N-Q2 allows 18 Q×N.N8+ N-B1 19 Q×N+ winning a piece.

18	Q×N+	B-K1
19	N-B7+	K-Q2
20	Q-N4+	

and Black can resign because the queens are being exchanged.

B

1 P-K4 P-K4 2 N-KB3 P-KB4 3 B-B4 P×P 4 N×P Q-N4 5 P-Q4! Q×P
6 Q-R5+ P-KN3 7 B-B7+ K-Q1 8 B×P Q×R+ 9 K-K2

9...		P-B3(!)(*28*)

28

This move, although not objectively satisfactory, is relatively best. It is the suggestion of the German analysist Gerhard Gunderam and has been extensively analysed in *The Latvian Gambit Monthly* during the past few years.

>10   N-QB3   N-B3
>11   Q-B5!

This move was played in the simultaneous game Keres-N.N. at Siegen during the 1970 Olympiad. I glanced at the game briefly but at the time was unable to obtain a score sheet with the moves. Almost three months later I met Keres at the Palma Interzonal tournament and asked him about the game. Amazingly, he remembered the ideas that he had while he was playing it and he showed me the following analysis.

>11 ...   R-N1

If 11...B-K2 12 B-B4!! Q×R 13 N-B7+ K-K1 14 N×R+ K-Q1 (if 14...P×B 15 Q×P+ K-Q1 16 N-B7+ K-K1 17 N-Q6++ K-Q1 18 Q-K8+ N×Q 19 N-B7 mate) 15 N-B7+ K-K1 16 B-B7 and White wins. e.g. 16...P-Q4 17 N-K5+ K-B1 18 Q×B+ K-N1 19 B×RP+ N×B 20Q-N6+ and mate next move.

>12   Q×N+   B-K2

Not 12...K-B2 13 B-B4±±

>13   Q-B7

Threatening 14 B-N5 as well as 14 Q×R+

>13   ...   R×B

If 13...R-B1 14 Q×R+ B×Q 15 B-N5+ K-B2 16 R×Q P×B 17 N×KP with an easily won ending.

>14   B-N5   Q-B6+!

Forced, since 14...Q×R allows 15 Q×B+ K-B2 16 Q-Q8+ K-Q3 17 N-B4+ K-K3 18 Q-K7+ K-B4 19 N-K3 mate.

>15   N×Q   P×N+
>16   K×P   R×B

Not 16...B×B? 17 Q×RP and Black loses a piece.

>17   R-K1

and Black cannot move his bishop without losing his rook to 18 Q-B6+

C

1 P-K4 P-K4 2 N-KB3 P-KB4 3 B-B4 P×P 4 N×P Q-N4 5 P-Q4! Q×P 6 Q-R5+ P-KN3 7 B-B7+ K-Q1 8 B×P Q×R+ 9 K-K2

>9   ...   Q×B(29)

29

| 10 | N-B7+ | K-K1 |
| 11 | N×R+ | P×B |

11...K-Q1 fails to 12 Q-R4+ e.g. 12...B-K2 13 N-B7+ K-K1 14 Q×RP±± or 12...N-K2 13 Q-B6 B-N2 14 Q×B N×B 15 Q-N8+ K-K2 16 Q×P+ and Black will soon be mated.

12	Q×P+	K-Q1
13	N-B7+!	K-K2
14	N-B3!	

Threatening mate by 15 N-Q5.

| 14 | ... | Q×P+ |
| 15 | K-K1 | P-Q3 |

Black has no satisfactory defence. e.g.

a) 15...N-KB3 16 N-K5 P-B3 (or 16...K-K3 17 Q-B7+ K-B4 18 N-Q5±±) 17 Q-B7+ K-Q1 18 Q×B+ K-B2 19 N-B7 and Black is in a mating net—19...P-N4 20 Q-Q8+

b) 15...P-B3 16 N-Q6! (Threatening 17 Q-K8+!) 16...N-KB3 (if 16...K-Q1 17 Q×N K-B2 18 Q×B±±) 17 Q-N5! K-Q1 (or 17...B-N2 18 N3×P±±) 18 Q×N+ B-K2 (or.18...K-B2 19 N-Q5+ mating.) 19 Q-R8+ K-B2 20 N-Q5+, and Black must give up his queen to prevent mate.

16	N-Q5+	K-Q2
17	Q×N	Q×NP
18	R-Q1	

Black is helpless. 18...B-K2 allows 19 Q-N4+ K-K1 20 Q×B+ K×N 21 Q-B5+, and if 21...K-K1? 22 Q-K6+ mating. 18...P-B3 is no better: 19 N-K5+! QP×N 20 Q-B7+ K-Q3 21 P×P+ K-B4 22 Q×B+ ±±.

The reader will have noticed that our discussion of the Greco-Counter-Gambit is literally full of variations which end in a position that is winning for White. This is not because of any overstatement on our part but due to the complete unsoundness of the gambit. Keres' analysis puts the opening in its correct perspective and the reader who learns it thoroughly will be absolutely certain of winning against it, almost by force!

5 Queen's Pawn Counter Gambit

1 P-K4 P-K4   2 N-KB3 P-Q4 (*30*)

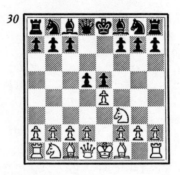

This is not so much a defence as a joke.

          3 P×P   P-K5

After 3...Q×P 4 N-B3 Q-K3 5 B-N5+ Black's development will be hampered by the exposed position of his queen.

          4 Q-K2   P-KB4

4...N-KB3 is met by 5 P-Q3 B-K2 (or 5...Q×P 6 KN-Q2±) 6 P×P O-O 7 Q-B4± (Black has little, if any, compensation for his pawns) and 4...Q-K2 by 5 N-Q4 Q-K4 (on 5...N-KB3 Pachman suggests 6 N-QB3 Q-K4 7 N-B3 Q-K2 8 N-KN5±) 6 N-N5 B-Q3 7 P-Q4 Q-K2 8 P-QB4 when White has a winning position, Morphy-Mongredien, Paris 1859.

          5 P-Q3   N-KB3

If 5...Q×P 6 QN-Q2 N-KB3 7 N-N5±

          6 P×P   P×P
          7 N-B3

White has a safe extra pawn. The game Tal-Lutikov, Tallinn 1964, concluded: 7...B-QN5 8 Q-N5+ P-B3 9 Q×B P×N 10 B-KN5 (returning the pawn for a crushing lead in development) 10...P×QP 11 O-O-O N-

B3 12 Q-R3 B-K3 13 B-QB4 Q-K2 14 N×P Q×Q 15 N-B7+ K-K2 16 KR-K1! Q-B4 17 R×B+ K-B1 18 R×N.KB6+ P×R 19 N-K6+ K-K2 20 N×Q P×B 21 R-Q7+ K-B3 22 R-Q6+ K-K2 23 R-K6+ K-Q1 24 N×P+ K-B2 25 R-Q5 and White soon won.

6 Sicilian Defence

1 P-K4 P-QB4

This is the most popular defence to 1 P-K4 at all levels of play. Most opponents who choose the Sicilian arrive at the board primed with current master systems and may know several difficult variations for twenty moves or more. Against the Sicilian we recommend the move 2 P-QB3 which was originally named Alapin's Variation but which normally transposes to the Smith-Morra Gambit Declined (1 P-K4 P-QB4 2 P-Q4 P×P 3 P-QB3 N-KB3).

This system has not been exhaustively analysed and it is not easy for Black to get a satisfactory game. With accurate play Black may be able to hold how own but White has chances of taking control of the centre and driving Black into a passive set-up.

1 P-K4	P-QB4
2 P-QB3 *(31)*	

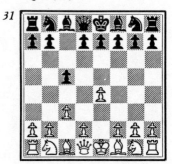

31

Black now has three serious alternatives:

A 2...N-KB3

B 2...P-Q4

C 2...P-K3

There are two other less important tries which the repertoire player should know how to refute:

a) 2...P-Q3 3 P-Q4 N-KB3? (relatively best is 3...P×P 4 P×P with some advantage to White because of his centre and easy development) 4 P×P!

P×P (4...N×P? 5 Q-R4+ loses a piece, while the counter-gambit 4...N-B3 5 P×P N×P 6 P×P Q×Q+ 7 K×Q B×P 8 B-K3 B-K3 9 N-B3 is not quite sound, Heidenfeld-Bennett, South African Ch 1955) 5 Q×Q+ K×Q leaves Black with poor prospects. Heidenfeld-Grzeskowiak, Frankfurt-am-Main 1960, continued 6 P-B3 N-B3 7 B-QB4 P-K3 8 N-KR3 B-Q2 9 B-K3 N-K4 10 B-K2 B-K2 11 N-Q2 P-KR3 12 N-B2 P-KN4 13 N-QN3 P-N3 14 O-O-O and Black has a difficult game.

b) 2...P-KN3 3 N-KB3! (this position can also arise from 1 P-K4 P-QB4 2 N-KB3 P-KN3 3 P-B3) 3...B-N2 (not 3...P-Q4? 4 P×P Q×P 5 P-Q4 B-N2 6 P×P Q×BP 7 B-K3; nor 3...N-KB3 4 P-K5 N-Q4 5 N-N5!! P-K3—or 5...Q-B2 6 P-Q4 P×P 7 P×P±—6 P-Q4 P×P 7 N-K4! B-K2 8 P×P P-B4 9 N4-B3 P-Q3 10 N×N P×N 11 B-QN5+ B-Q2 12 N-B3±) 4 P-Q4 P×P 5 P×P P-Q4 (the only active move) 6 P-K5 B-N5 7 B-QN5+ N-Q2 8 QN-Q2 P-K3 9 O-O N-K2 10 P-KR3 B×N 11 N×B± Matulovic-Parma, Skopje-Ohrid 1968.

Á

1 P-K4 P-QB4 2 P-QB3

2 ...	N-KB3

This is the most commonly seen defence to 2 P-QB3. Black attacks White's KP, encouraging it to advance so that the KN will be able to use the Q4 square.

3 P-K5	N-Q4
4 P-Q4	P×P
5 B-QB4	

Now there are two major alternatives:

A1 5...Q-B2
A2 5...N-N3

A1

1 P-K4 P-QB4 2 P-QB3 N-KB3 3 P-K5 N-Q4 4 P-Q4 P×P 5 B-QB4

5 ...	Q-B2 *(32)*

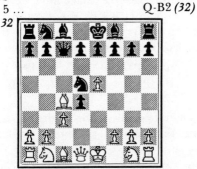

This move of the late Yugoslav international master Rabar is considered Black's strongest but the repertoire player can face it with confidence. It gives White at worst a promising gambit at the price of a pawn, while if Black chooses an inferior line he can easily get crushed. For instance, after the passive 5...P-K3 6 P×P P-Q3 7 N-KB3 N-QB3 8 O-O B-K2 9 Q-K2, White's pawn wedge at K5 gives him easy attacking chances against the black king. A game Steinberg-Soltis, New York 1970, concluded 9...O-O 10 R-Q1 P-QR3 11 N-B3 N3-N5 12 N-K4 N-N3 13 B-N3 P-Q4 14 N-N3 B-Q2 15 N-K1 P-QR4 16 B-Q2 P-R5 17 B×N (this move results in all Black's minor pieces being cut off from his beleaguered K-side) 17...B×B 18 B-B2 N-B5 19 N-R5 Q-N4 20 R-Q3 Q-K2 21 N-B6+! P×N 22 R-KN3+ K-R1 23 B×KRP B×N 24 Q-R5 1-O.

6 Q-K2	N-N3
7 B-Q3	N-B3

If 7...P-K3 8 N-B3 P-Q3 9 KP×P B×P 10 N×P P-QR3 11 N-B5!±

8 N-B3	P-K3

8...P-Q4 is recommended for Black in many textbooks but an analysis in *Chess Correspondent*, September 1970, shows that it is really good for White after 9 KP×Pep Q×P 10 O-O P-N3 (10...P×P 11 N×P P-QR3 12 R-Q1 gives Black a headache in return for an extra pawn) 11 N×P N×N 12 P×N B-N2 13 N-B3 and now:

a) 13...O-O 14 B-K3 B×P? 15 N-N5 Q-N5 16 B×B R-Q1 17 B-B3 1-0 (Evans-Keller, corres 1962); or

b) 13...P-QR3 14 B-KN5 P-K3? 15 N-K4 Q×QP 16 B-K3 Q-Q1 17 B-QB5 with a winning attack. Melton-Beckwith, corres 1967

Relatively best for Black in this variation seems 10...P-K3 (instead of 10...P-N3) but then 11 P×P B-K2 12 R-Q1 B-Q2 13 N-B3 O-O 14 N-K4 gives White promising attacking chances.

9 O-O	P-Q3

Many players with black will accept the gambit pawn in such positions and hope to survive the attack after 9...P×P 10 N×P P-QR3. The game might continue 11 B-KB4 B-K2 12 QR-B1 O-O 13 Q-K4 P-N3 14 B-R6 R-K1 15 Q-KB4 and White is already threatening 16 N-K4 with a quick crunch on the dark squares.

10	BP×P	P×P
11	P×P	N-Q2
12	B-KB4	

White's space control and his opportunities for rook play on the open QB-file give him a clear positional advantage. Analysis by Smith.

A2

1 P-K4 P-QB4 2 P-QB3 N-KB3 3 P-K5 N-Q4 4 P-Q4 P×P 5 B-QB4

5 ...		N-N3(*33*)

33

| 6 B-N3 | P-Q3 |

6...P×P 7 N×P N-B3 8 N-B3 P-Q3 9 P×P threatening 10 N-KN5 gives White excellent attacking chances.

6...P-Q4 7 P×P N-B3 8 N-K2 B-N5 9 P-B3 B-B4 10 QN-B3 P-K3 11 O-O followed by the advance of the KBP is also strong for White. Radoicic-O'Kelly, Bognor 1957, continued 11...P-QR3 12 N-N3 B-N3 13 P-B4 N-K2 14 P-QR4 P-KR4 15 P-R5 P-R5 16 P-B5!±

| 7 N-B3 | N-B3 |
| 8 KP×P | Q×P |

It is easy for Black to go astray, e.g. 8...QP×P? 9 N×P P×P (or 9...Q×P 10 Q×Q P×Q 11 N-QN5) 10 N-KN5 P-Q4 11 O-O B-K2 12 Q-R5 P-N3 13 Q-R6 B-B1 14 R-K1+ with a winning attack. Milner-Barry-Van den Berg, England-Holland match 1960, continued 14...N-K2 15 Q-R4 B-N2 16 B-K3 P-KR3 17 B×N P×B 18 N×QP! P×N 19 Q-N3 B-K3 and now 20 N-B7+ would have won quickly.

9 P×P	B-B4
10 N-B3	P-K3
11 O-O	B-K2
12 P-Q5	P×P
13 N×P	N×N
14 Q×N	Q×Q
15 B×Q	O-O
16 B-N5	B×B
17 N×B	

White has a very slight endgame advantage. Milner-Barry — Darga, Bognor 1961.

B

1 P-K4 P-QB4 2 P-QB3

| 2 ... | P-Q4 (*34*) |

34

This central counter looks logical since White's QB3 square is occupied by a pawn and so White is unable to take immediate advantage of the position of Black's queen. However, White still has the initiative and it will not be long before Black's queen *does* feel exposed in the middle of the board.

3 P×P	Q×P
4 P-Q4	N-QB3

4...P-K3 5 N-B3 N-QB3 transposes to variation B1 as does 4...P-K3 5 N-B3 N-KB3 6 B-K2 N-B3 (but not 6...P×P 7 P×P B-N5+ 8 N-B3 O-O 9 O-O Q-Q1 10 N-K5 when White has chances of a K-side attack and Black's Q-side development is lagging).

There are two other simplifying tries, both involving the move . . .P-K4:

a) 4...P-K4? 5 P×KP Q×KP+ 6 B-K2 N-QB3 7 N-B3 Q-Q3 8 Q-R4 B-Q2 9 B-KB4± Perlis-Tartakower, 1908.

b) 4...P×P 5 P×P P-K4 6 B-K3 P×P 7 N-QB3 Q-QR4 8 B×P N-QB3 9 B-N5 B-Q2 10 Q-K2+! KN-K2 11 N-B3 O-O-O 12 O-O N×B 13 N×N± Janosevic-Primavera, San Benedetto 1955. In both games Black suffered through having his queen hunted around too much.

There are also two more complex alternatives:

c) 4...P×P 5 P×P N-KB3 (5...N-QB3 transposes to B2) 6 N-QB3 is also good for White. e.g. 6...Q-QR4 7 N-B3 P-K3 8 B-Q3 B-Q3 9 O-O QN-Q2 10 N-QN5 B-N1 11 B-Q2 Q-N3 12 Q-K1 P-QR4 13 P-QR4 O-O 14 P-QN4± Yukhtman-Zlotnik, USSR 1959. White threatens to drive Black's pieces from pillar to post, e.g. 14...P×P 15 B×NP R-K1 16 P-R5.

d) 4...N-KB3 5 N-B3 B-N5 6 B-K2 P-K3 7 O-O B-K2 is met by 8 Q-R4+ N-B3 9 R-Q1 O-O 10 P×P with a big initiative.

5 N-B3

And now:

B1 5...*P-K3*
B2 5...*P×P*
B3 5...*B-N5*

B1

1 P-K4 P-QB4 2 P-QB3 P-Q4 3 P×P Q×P 4 P-Q4 N-QB3 5 N-B3

5 ...   P-K3 (*35*)

6 B-Q3	N-B3
7 O-O	B-K2

Also good for White is 7...P×P 8 P×P B-K2 9 N-B3 Q-Q3 (or 9...Q-Q1 10 B-K3 N-QN5 11 B-N1 O-O 12 N-K5 B-Q2 13 Q-B3 B-B3 14 Q-R3 with fair attacking chances, Gipslis-Baumbach, Bad Liebenstein 1963) 10 Q-K2 O-O 11 R-Q1 N-Q4 12 Q-K4 P-B4 13 Q-K1 B-B3 14 B-QB4, Zhuravlev-Karpov, RSFSR ch 1971, is rather better for White as he can keep Black's KP backward.

8 P-B4	Q-Q1
9 P×P	O-O
10 N-B3	B×P
11 B-N5	B-K2
12 Q-K2	Q-R4
13 N-K4	N×N
14 B×B	N×B
15 B×N	P-B3
16 KR-Q1±	

Zak-Krasnov, USSR 1973.

B2

1 P-K4 P-QB4 2 P-QB3 P-Q4 3 P×P Q×P 4 P-Q4 N-QB3 5 N-B3

5 ...   P×P
6 P×P (*36*)

36

6 ...   B-N5

If 6...P-K4 7 N-B3 B-QN5 8 B-Q2 B×N 9 B×B P-K5 (or 9...P×P 10 N×P N×N 11 Q×N Q×Q 12 B×Q and White still has a slight plus because of the two bishops) 10 N-K5 N×N 11 P×N N-K2 12 Q-R4+ B-Q2 13 Q-N4 followed by 14 B-QB4 with the initiative.

Or 6...P-K3 7 N-B3 B-N5 8 B-K2 N-B3 9 O-O Q-Q1 10 B-KN5 B-K2 11 R-B1 O-O 12 B-Q3 Letzelter-Huguet, France 1968. White has the freer position.

7 N-B3!

Euwe's move. 7 B-K2 transposes to B3.

7 ...   B×N

There is no viable alternative. e.g.

a) 7...Q-Q3 8 P-Q5 N-K4 9 B-QN5+ B-Q2 (or 9...N-Q2 10 P-KR3 B-R4 11 P-KN4 B-N3 12 Q-R4±) 10 B-KB4! B×B 11 B×N Q-R3 12 N-Q4 and Black's development is severely lacking, I. Zaitsev-Koifman, USSR 1968

b) 7...Q-QR4? 8 P-Q5 N-K4 (or 8...O-O-O 9 B-Q2 N-K4 10 Q-B1! Q-B2 11 N-QN5±±) 9 N×N! B×Q 10 B-QN5+ K-Q1 11 N×P+ K-B1 12 K×B winning. Kirillov-Skuja, Latvia 1965.

8 P×B   Q×QP

Not 8...Q-QR4? 9 P-Q5 O-O-O 10 Q-N3±

9 Q×Q   N×Q
10 N-N5!   P-K4

The alternatives have long been known to favour White:

a) 10...N-B7+? 11 K-Q1 N×R 12 N-B7+ K-Q2 13 N×R P-K4 14 B-K3 P-QN3 15 B-QR6! when Black's knight is trapped while White's cannot readily be attacked.

b) 10...N×N? 11 B×N+ K-Q1 12 B-KB4±

c) 10...O-O-O 11 N×N R×N 12 B-K3±

d) 10...N-K3 11 B-K3 P-QR3 12 O-O-O ±. In each case White's quicker development guarantees an advantage.

11	N-B7+	K-Q2
12	N×R	B-N5+
13	K-Q1	N-K2
14	B-K3	N2-B3
15	B-QB4	

Black has insufficient play to compensate for his material deficit.

B3

1 P-K4 P-QB4 2 P-QB3 P-Q4 3 P×P Q×P 4 P-Q4 N-QB3 5 N-B3

5 ...   B-N5(*37*)

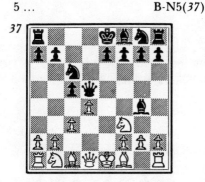

This is Black's best chance. By delaying the exchange . . .P×P for one move Black prevents his opponent from meeting . . .B-N5 with N-B3 (as in variation B2).

6 B-K2   P×P

6...O-O-O? is very dangerous—Black's Q-side is extremely vulnerable: 7 P×P Q×BP (the exchange of queens is scarcely better) 8 Q-R4 B×N 9 B×B N-Q5 10 P×N Q×B+ 11 K-K2 Q×P+ (11...Q×R? 12 Q×P) 12 N-Q2 Q×QP 13 KR-QB1+ K-N1 14 Q-B2 with a powerful attack, Yudovich-Lyubitel, corres 1959.

Also bad is 6...P-K4, e.g. 7 P×KP B×N 8 B×B Q×Q+ 9 B×P 10 B-R4+ with the two bishops.

6...P-K3 can be met by 7 P-B4 (7 O-O P×P 8 P×P transposes to the text) 7...Q-Q2 8 P-Q5! P×P 9 P×P and now:

a) 9...N-N5? 10 N-B3 O-O-O 11 O-O B-Q3 12 P-QR3 B×N 13 P×N B×B 14 Q×B K-N1 15 P×P B×BP 16 B-B4+ ± Altschuler-Barkhatov, Moscow 1960. Here too White has a strong attack.

b) 9...B×N 10 B×B N-Q5 11 O-O N×B+ (if 11...N-KB3 12 N-B3 B-K2 13 B-K3 with a very active game, Angelov-Christov, Bulgarian Corres Ch 1961-2) 12 Q×N B-Q3 13 N-B3 N-K2. According to Schwarz this position is level but in reality White is better. He has a strong passed pawn and the more active development. One possible continuation is 14 B-B4 B×B 15 Q×B O-O (not 15...N×P?? 16 Q-K5+) 16 QR-Q1 ±

| 7 P×P | P-K3 |

Not 7...P-K4? 8 N-B3 Q-QR4 9 P×P B×N 10 B×B Q×KP+ 11 B-K3 B-B4 12 O-O B-K2 13 R-K1 and Black is in trouble (the K-file).

8 O-O	N-B3
9 N-B3	Q-Q2
10 N-K5	B×B
11 N×Q	B×Q
12 N×N+	P×N
13 R×B	O-O-O
14 B-K3	B-N5

So far we have been following the game Matulovic-Trifunovic, Yugoslav Ch 1958. Now, with 15 P-Q5! B×N 16 P×N B×P 17 P×P+, White could have maintained his advantage.

C

1 P-K4 P-QB4 2 P-QB3

| 2 ... | P-K3 *(38)* |

38

This reply is rarely seen because White may force his opponent into the French Defence and the solid French is not normally to the taste of lively Sicilian addicts.

| 3 P-Q4 | P-Q4 |
| 4 KP×P | |

4 P-K5 transposes to the Advance Variation of the French.

| 4 ... | KP×P |

4...Q×P transposes to variation B (note to Black's fourth move).

| 5 N-B3 | N-QB3 |

Imprecise is 5...N-KB3 6 B-QN5+ N-B3 7 O-O B-K2 8 P×P B×P 9 B-N5 B-K3 10 QN-Q2, when White will soon post a knight on Q4.

6 B-QN5	B-Q3
7 O-O	KN-K2

If 7...P×P 8 Q×P! N-B3 9 Q-QR4 O-O 10 B×N P×B 11 Q×BP B-KN5 12 QN-Q2 R-B1 13 Q-R4 B-N1 14 P-KR3 B-R4 15 N-Q4, and Black has nothing to show for the sacrificed pawn, Minev-Gligoric, Amsterdam Olympiad 1954.

8 P×P	B×BP
9 QN-Q2	O-O
10 N-N3	B-N3

If 10...B-Q3 11 N.N3-Q4 effecting a blockade on Black's isolated pawn.

11 R-K1	B-KB4

If 11...B-N5 12 B-N5 Q-Q3 13 Q-Q3. In all these lines White has good play against Black's isolated QP.

12 B-K3	B-K5
13 N.N3-Q4	Q-Q3
14 B-KB1	Q-B3
15 Q-R4	P-KR3
16 QR-Q1±	

Ghizdavu-Botez, Romania 1972.

7 French Defence

1 P-K4   P-K3

A favourite weapon with Botvinnik and Uhlmann, the French has endured the passage of time and emerged with the stamp of respectability accorded to very few opening systems. It is often underrated as being too passive but this is very far from the truth. Black has two traditional thematic ideas, the break . . .P-QB4 putting pressure on White's QP and, where appropriate, . . .P-KB3 to attack the white pawn that so often advances to K5. Each of these breaks carries with it the possibility of an attack along a bishop's file and in the long term they often bring about the exchange of White's central pawns and thereby lead to positions in which Black's pawns at K3 and Q4 are able to advance with considerable effect.

After White's most active third move (3 N-QB3) there is no one system that will satisfy all of Black's possible replies. We must therefore treat each of these replies on its own merit.

2 P-Q4   P-Q4

Larsen has recently been experimenting with the 'Franco-Sicilian' 2...P-QB4 which gives White the option of transposing to the Sicilian Defence proper with 3 N-KB3. A more ambitious try is 3 P-Q5 PxP 4 PxP P-Q3 5 N-KB3, when White retains some advantage. e.g. 5...B-N5 6 B-K2 BxN 7 BxB B-K2 8 O-O N-KB3 9 N-R3! O-O 10 N-B4 QN-Q2 11 R-K1! (Gligoric).

3 N-QB3

The most active move. Unlike most of today's grandmasters who prefer Tarrasch's quieter 3 N-Q2, Fischer almost always plays 3 N-QB3.

We have now reached an important parting of the ways and it is necessary to examine these variations in some detail:

A 3...B-N5

B 3...PxP

C 3...N-KB3

If 3...P-QB4? 4 KPxP KPxP (on 4...BPxP?, 5 B-QN5+ wins a pawn, e.g. 5...B-Q2 6 Q×P B×B 7 N×B P×P 8 Q×QP!) 5 P×P! gives White an excellent game. e.g. 5...P-Q5 (or 5...N-KB3 6 B-K3!) 6 B-QN5+ N-QB3 7 B×N+ P×B 8 N3-K2! B×P 9 N-KB3 and now:

a) 9...B-KN5? 10 N.B3×P with a good pawn extra;

b) 9...B-QN5+ 10 B-Q2 B×B+ 11 Q×B P-QB4 12 O-O-O±;

c) 9...Q-Q4 10 O-O B-KN5 11 N.B3×P B.B4×N 12 Q×B B×N 13 Q×Q P×Q 14 R-K1 and White has again won a pawn; or

d) 9...Q-R4+ 10 B-Q2 Q-N3 11 O-O (threatening 12 P-QN4) 11...P-QR4 (if 11...B-R3 12 P-QN4 B×N 13 Q×B+ B-K2 14 Q-B4 again winning a pawn, or 11...Q×P 12 R-K1 N-K2 13 N2×P!±± 12 R-K1 B-K3 13 N-B4 and White has an enormous position.

3...N-QB3 transposes to Nimzowitsch's Defence. (see page XXX).

A

1 P-K4 P-K3 2 P-Q4 P-Q4 3 N-QB3   3 ...   B-N5 *(39)*

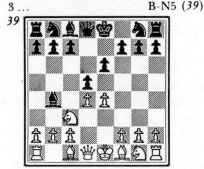

The Winawer Variation, Black's most dynamic defence (attack!?) and the prime reason for the popularity of Tarrasch's 3 N-Q2. Most of the analysis performed on the Winawer in recent years has been devoted to the well known line 4 P-K5 P-QB4 5 P-QR3 B×N+ 6 P×B. Here we shall examine a sharper system once championed by Alekhine. It found favour with Smyslov in his 1954 World Championship match against Botvinnik and has recently been tried on a couple of occasions by Bobby Fischer.

4 P-QR3

The idea of this move is to reach a position similar to those arising in the main line (4 P-K5 P-QB4 5 P-QR3 B×N+ 6 P×B) but in which the tactics start *before* Black has had time to play . . .P-QB4. As with many lines of the Winawer, White grabs Black's KNP and thereby wrecks Black's K-side, but the difference here is that Black's counterplay takes longer than usual to get going.

                4 ...   B×N+

4...B-R4 5 P-QN4 B-N3 6 P-K5 gives White a superior form of the
Winawer Variation inasmuch as Black will never have time enough to
force . . .P-QB4. Play might continue 6...N-K2 7 Q-N4 N-B4 8 N-B3
P-KR4 (if 8...O-O 9 B-Q3±) 9 Q-B4 followed by B-Q3±, when Black
has no counterplay.

    5 P×B   P×P

Logical and best. 5...P-QB4 can be met by 6 KP×P KP×P 7 P×P!? N-
KB3 8 B-Q3 O-O 9 N-K2 QN-Q2 10 B-K3 Q-B2 11 B-Q4±. Foltys-
Opocensky, 1938. White has considerable pressure against Black's K-
side.

Instead of utilizing this option White may, if he wishes transpose
back to the text by (5...P-QB4) 6 Q-N4 N-B3 7 Q×NP R-N1 8 Q-R6
QP×P.
    5...N-K2 should be met by Keres' interesting but untried suggestion 6
B-Q3.

    6 Q-N4   N-KB3

6...Q-B3? was exposed as unsound (by 7 Q×P.K4) during the last
century e.g. 7...N-K2 8 B-KB4 P-B3 9 B-K5 Q-B4 10 B-Q3 when Black
is obliged to exchange queens leaving White with the two bishops and
much the better development, (Huch-Manvide, 1872); or 7... N-B3 8
N-B3 KN-K2 9 B-Q3± (Walbrodt-Noa, 1896). The black queen is
misplaced on the K-side.

    7 Q×NP   R-N1
    8 Q-R6 (*40*)

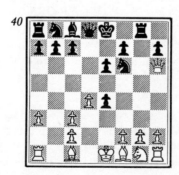

We have now reached a critical position in which it is necessary to
consider four possible moves.

A1 8...P-N3
A2 8...QN-Q2
A3 8...P-B4
A4 8...R-N3
A1

1 P-K4 P-K3 2 P-Q4 P-Q4 3 N-QB3 B-N5 4 P-QR3 BxN+ 5 PxB PxP
6 Q-N4 N-KB3 7 QxNP R-N1 8 Q-R6

| 8 ... | P-N3 |

A relatively unexplored move.

9 B-KN5	R-N3
10 Q-R4	B-N2
11 N-K2!	P-KR3

If 11...QN-Q2 12 N-B4 R-KN1 13 N-R5 R-N3 14 NxN+ NxN 15 B-
K2(±) followed by B-R5 winning the exchange.

12 BxP

White has gained an important pawn and because of his passed KRP
almost any endgame will be an attractive proposition.

| 12 ... | Q-Q4 |

Maric considers this move to be dubious but fails to suggest any
alternative. White is 'threatening' 13 P-KR3 (13 N-B4? R-N5) followed
by 14 N-B4 R-KN1 15 B-KN5 and 16 N-R5 winning a piece because of
the pin on Black's KN. 12...Q-B1 does not help matters because White
can then play 13 B-N5 KN-Q2 (if 13...QN-Q2, 14 N-B4 wins a piece.)
14 Q-R8+ N-B1 15 B-R6 N-Q2 16 N-B4 winning the exchange.

13 N-B4

Also possible is 13 B-Q2 after which White has a clear advantage
because of his extra pawn, two active bishops and the simultaneous
threats of 14 N-B4 and 14 Q-R8+ N-N1 15 P-KR4.

| 13 ... | Q-QR4 |
| 14 B-QN5+! | QxB! |

Not 14...P-B3 15 NxR QxBP+ 16 K-K2 QxBP+ 17 B-Q2 when
White is winning.

15 NxR

The brittle structure on Black's K-side has at last given way.

| 15 ... | B-R3 |

Threatening mate in one!

| 16 N-B4 | Q-N7 |
| 17 QxN | QxP.B6+ |

Black cannot afford to capture the rooks because his king is weak: (17...Q×R+ 18 K-Q2 Q×R) 19 N×P! and Black is soon mated.

18	K-Q1	N-Q2
19	Q-R8+	K-K2

So far we have been following the game Watson-Whiteley, British Championship 1968. Now White should have continued forcefully with 20 N-N6+! P×N (20...K-Q3?? 21 B-B4+ K-B3 22 Q×R+ ±±) 21 B-N5+ K-Q3 22 B-B4+ K-K2 (not 22...K-B3?? 23 P-Q5+ winning the queen) 23 Q-N7+ K-Q1 24 R-QN1± (analysis by Maric). White has won the exchange and still retains an attack.

A2

1 P-K4 P-K3 2 P-Q4 P-Q4 3 N-QB3 B-N5 4 P-QR3 B×N+ 5 P×B P×P 6 Q-N4 N-KB3 7 Q×NP R-N1 8 Q-R6

8 ...		QN-Q2 (*41*)

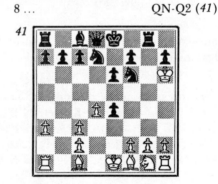

This move is also rarely seen-it exploded into fame when an unknown Yugoslav (Kovacevic) used it in a game which he won from Fischer at Zagreb 1970.

9 N-K2	P-QB4

In the Fischer-Kovacevic game Black played 9...P-QN3 when 10 N-N3 would have been correct (with the plan of 11 B-K2 and 12 O-O). If then 10...B-N2, White can continue with 11 B-KN5 followed by N-R5 as in variation A1 (note to Black's 11th move).

We have now transposed to variation A3 (note to Black's 9th move).

A3

1 P-K4 P-K3 2 P-Q4 P-Q4 3 N-QB3 B-N5 4 P-QR3 B×N+ 5 P×B P×P 6 Q-N4 N-KB3 7 Q×NP R-N1 8 Q-R6

8 ...	P-B4
9 N-K2	R-N3

9...QN-Q2 can be met by 10 N-N3 and now:

a) 10...Q-R4 11 B-Q2 P-N3 (11...Q-R5 12 PxP± — Alekhine) 12 P-QR4 PxP 13 PxP Q-Q4 produces a position in which, according to Keres, Black may have sufficient counterplay. After 14 Q-K3! B-N2 15 P-KR3! however, I think that White's advantage is still there — he has adequate control of the centre and good prospects of creating play against Black's weak king.

b) 10 ...P-N3? 11 B-QN5! R-N3 12 Q-K3 Q-B2 13 PxP PxP 14 NxP NxN 15 QxN B-N2 16 Q-KB4 P-K4 17 Q-KR4 BxP 18 R-KN1 Q-R4 19 BxN+ KxB 20 B-N2 QR-KN1 21 O-O-O with a terrific attack. Fichtl-Altschul, 1956

c) 10...R-N3? 11 Q-K3 N-Q4 12 QxP NxP 13 Q-Q3 N-Q4 14 B-K2 Q-B3 (or 14...PxP 15 QxP Q-B3 16 QxQ±) 15 P-QB3± Alekhine-Euwe, 3rd match game 1935, continued: 15...PxP 16 PxP N2-N3 (if 16...N-B5 17 BxN QxB 18 O-O±) 17 B-R5! R-N2 18 B-B3 (threatening 19 N-R5) 18...Q-N3 19 B-K4! P-B4 20 B-B3 K-B1 21 P-QR4! R-QB2 22 O-O B-Q2 23 B-R3+ K-N1 24 P-R5 with a tremendous game for White.

d) 10...Q-B2 11 B-QN5! R-N3 (if 11...PxP? 12 QxN QxBP+ 13 K-Q1 QxR 14 NxP and White wins. 13...R-N3 is no real improvement either because of 14 Q-R8+ K-K2 15 R-QN1! N-B3 16 R-N3 Q-B4 17 P-QR4! winning. In many of the variations hereabouts Black loses becuase his king is so unsafe.) 12 Q-Q2 P-QR3 13 B-K2 P-N3 14 O-O B-N2 15 P-B3± Bloch-Huss, Siegen Olympiad 1970.

9...B-Q2 is answered by 10 B-KN5! R-N3 11 Q-R4 B-B3 12 P-Q5!

9...N-B3 10 PxP R-N3 11 Q-Q2 transposes to the text.

10   Q-Q2!   N-QB3

After 10...QN-Q2, White can try Keres' interesting suggestion, 11 P-QB4. The idea behind this move is to prepare for P-Q5 (followed by N-B3), creating a useful passed pawn and attempting to prise open Black's king position.

11   PxP

It is somewhat rare for White to be able to afford the luxury of tripled pawns, particularly in the Winawer Variation. Normally White must maintain a pawn at Q4 so as to support its neighbour at K5. One advantage of White's whole system here is that there is no KP to be protected. Consequently, Black has no immediate counterplay that can be used as a reprisal for 11 PxP.

11   ...   B-Q2

11...QxQ+ would be a grave error since without queens on the board Black will find it extremely difficult to attack White's advanced QBP. The triplets would then be very useful for White because between them they control a number of important squares.

12	R-QN1	Q-B2
13	Q-Q6!	O-O-O
14	Q×Q+	K×Q

So White has managed to exchange queens but in doing so he has had to make the concession of leaving Black's king conveniently situated to watch over the QBPs.

This position was reached in the 19th game of the 1954 World Championship match (Smyslov-Botvinnik) and after the game Botvinnik recommended 15 N-N3 as strongest (±) with the idea of 16 B-K2 followed by O-O. Here we shall examine a few moves of the game itself as this will give the reader a good grasp of some of the ideas involved in the position.

15	N-Q4	P-QR3

To allow 16 N-N5+ K-N1 17 N-Q6 would be foolish.

16	B-KB4+	K-B1

Keres now suggests 17 B-Q6 as being the best way to increase the pressure, e.g. 17...N-K1 18 B-N3 or 17...N-Q4 18 K-Q2 and in each case White has almost complete control of the dark squares. 17 N×N B×N 18 P-B4 also leaves White with the advantage.

A4

1 P-K4 P-K3 2 P-Q4 P-Q4 3 N-QB3 B-N5 4 P-QR3 B×N+ 5 P×B P×P 6 Q-N4 N-KB3 7 Q×NP R-N1 8 Q-R6

8 ...   R-N3 *(42)*

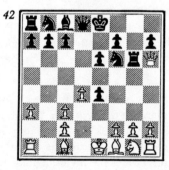

9 Q-Q2!   P-N3

If 9...N-B3 10 B-N2 N-K2, Keres' suggestion of 11 P-QB4 leaves White with the freer position (±)

9...P-B4 10 N-K2 N-B3 11 P×P transposes to variation A3.

10	B-N2	B-N2
11	O-O-O	Q-Q3

11...QN-Q2 followed by 12...Q-K2 has been suggested instead of the text. After 11...QN-Q2 White should continue with 12 P-B3 Q-K2 13 B-N5 (White's previous move left the KNP defended), and if 13...O-O-O then 14 Q-K2 with chances for both sides in the lively struggle ahead.

	12	P-B3	N-B3

Black's pawn at K5 is a useful possession because it controls White's KB3 and Q3 squares and thereby hinders the completion of White's development. For this reason the exchange 12...PxP 13 NxP can only be to White's advantage.

	13	Q-K1	O-O-O
	14	PxP	Q-B5+
	15	K-N1	QxKP
	16	N-B3	N-QR4

The position offers chances to both sides, Lutikov-Golz, Bad Salzungen 1960.

B

1 P-K4 P-K3 2 P-Q4 P-Q4 3 N-QB3

	3 ...		PxP

Rubinstein's Defence, which aims at simplification through early exchanges. With his third move Black cedes ground in the centre and the issue then revolves around the question of whether White can maintain his centre or whether he is forced into some equalizing exchanging sequences. Experience suggests that White should enjoy excellent prospects in this variation and games won by Spassky and Tal illustrate the kind of attack that White can sometimes build up against the black king.

4 NxP (*43*)

Black now has a variety of moves from which to choose. We shall divide our discussion into:

B1 4...B-K2

B2 4...B-Q2?!
B3 4...N-KB3
B4 4...N-Q2
B5 Other fourth moves

B1

1 P-K4 P-K3 2 P-Q4 P-Q4 3 N-QB3 P×P 4 N×P

4 ...   B-K2

Black prepares for . . .N-KB3 in such a way as to be able to recapture (after White's N×N+) with the bishop and thereby intensify his pressure on White's QP. The disadvantage of the text is that it does not pose White any immediate problems and the first player therefore has a free choice of moves with which to fortify his centre and/or prepare for an eventual K-side attack.

5 N-KB3   N-KB3

5...P-QN3 is much too slow. The game Fred-Sköld, 1951 continued 6 B-Q3 N-Q2 7 Q-K2 B-N2 8 O-O KN-B3 9 R-Q1! P-KR3 10 B-KB4 N-Q4 11 B-Q2(±) whereupon Sköld blundered and lost very quickly: 11...N-N5? 12 B×N B×B 13 P-Q5! P-K4 14 B-N5 B-Q3 15 N×B+ P×N 16 N×P P×N 17 Q×P+ K-B1 18 Q-Q6+ 1-0.

5...N-Q2 transposes to variation B4, note to Black's fifth move.

6 N×N+   B×N
7 B-Q3   N-B3

On 7...N-Q2 8 Q-K2 O-O (or 8...P-B4 9 P-Q5 Q-K2 10 P×P Q×P 11 Q×Q+ P×Q±) 9 B-K3, White gets good attacking chances after 9...R-K1 10 O-O-O P-B4 11 P-KR4! or 9...Q-K2 10 P-KR4!

7...P-B4 8 P×P Q-R4+ is best met by 9 B-Q2 Q×BP 10 O-O! and if 10...B×P then 11 R-N1 B-B3 (11...B-R6?? 12 R-N3±±) 12 B-N4 with a tremendous game for the pawn.

8 P-B3!

Securing White's centre still further.

8 ...   P-K4

If 8...O-O 9 Q-B2 P-KN3 10 B-KR6 followed by O-O-O and a K-side pawn storm.

9 P×P   N×P
10 N×N   B×N

The recent exchanges did little to help Black because White has remained with one very important advantage—on an open board he has the initiative.

11	O-O	B-Q3

Not 11...O-O? 12 B×P+ K×B 13 Q-R5+ regaining the piece and thereby winning a pawn.

12	R-K1+	B-K3
13	Q-R5	

Threatening 14 R×B+ as well as 14 Q-QN5+

13	...	Q-Q2
14	B-KN5	

Now Black cannot castle Q-side and White threatens 15 B-B5.

14	...	P-KN3
15	Q-R4	O-O

Black has solved the immediate problem of the safety of his king but White remains with the more active position. Paoli-Kottnauer, 1949.

B2

1 P-K4 P-K3 2 P-Q4 P-Q4 3 N-QB3 P×P 4 N×P

4...	B-Q2?!(*44*)

This move represents a completely unthematic idea in which Black plans to develop his bishop on the QR1-KR8 diagonal while evading the consequences of 4...P-QN3 (see B5). On QB3 Black's bishop blocks his QBP and it is then almost impossible for him to put pressure on White's QP in the usual way (...P-QB4).

44

5 N-KB3		B-B3
6 B-Q3		N-B3

Already Black has difficulty in completing his development. If 6...B×N 7 B×B P-QB3 8 O-O N-B3 9 B-Q3, White has an advantage in space and the two bishops. Spassky-O'Kelly, San Juan 1969, continued 9...QN-Q2 10 P-B4 B-Q3 11 P-QN3 O-O 12 B-N2 Q-B2 13 Q-B2± 6...N-Q2 leads to a similar sort of position. e.g. 7 Q-K2 KN-B3 8 O-O N×N 9 B×N B×B 10 Q×B P-QB3 11 P-B4 B-K2 12 P-QN3 O-O 13 B-N2

R-K1 14 QR-Q1± (Black is very cramped, but not necessarily losing) Shianovsky-Kostyuchenko, 'Avangard' tournament Kiev 1965.

7 N×N+   P×N

If 7...Q×N?? 8 B-KN5! B×N 9 Q-Q2 and Black loses his Queen (9...Q×P 10 B-N5+)

8 Q-K2±

B3

1 P-K4 P-K3 2 P-Q4 P-Q4 3 N-QB3 P×P 4 N×P

4 ...   N-KB3(*45*)

After an examination of the consequences of this move, the reader will come to understand why 4...N-Q2 (variation B4) has long been the main line.

5 N×N+   P×N

On 5...Q×N 6 N-B3, White threatens 7 B-KN5 followed by 8 B-Q3 with a colossal lead in development.

Black may then try:

a) 6...P-KR3 7 B-Q3 N-B3 (if 7...B-Q3 8 O-O O-O 9 Q-K2 N-B3 10 Q-K4 R-Q1 11 P-KN4! with a very strong attack) or 7...P-B4 8 B-K3± Janosevic-Puc, Yugoslavia 1948) 8 O-O B-Q3 9 P-B3 B-Q2 10 Q-K2 O-O-O 11 P-QN4! ± (analysis by Duckstein). White's attack will prove stronger than Black's because he can gain control of his K5 square, providing his knight with an outpost;

b) 6...Q-Q1 7 B-Q3 P-QB4 8 O-O P×P 9 N×P B-K2 10 B-KB4 gives White a handy lead in development, Hubner-Troger, West Germany 1964; or

c) 6...B-Q2? 7 B-KN5 Q-N3 8 B-Q3 P-KB4 9 P-KR4! N-B3 10 Q-K2 P-KR3 11 B-KB4 O-O-O 12 O-O-O B-Q3 13 B-K5!± Tarrasch-Lasker, 6th match game 1908.

6 N-B3   P-QN3

6...P-B3?! was tried in the game Glauser-Troger, Clare Benedict

Cup, Adelboden 1969. After 7 B-Q3 B-Q3 8 Q-K2 Q-B2 9 B-Q2 N-Q2 10 O-O-O P-N3, Black's game was very cramped and White had fine prospects on both sides of the board. The game concluded: 11 N-R4! B-N2 12 Q-R5 N-B1 13 Q-R6! R-KN1 14 KR-K1 O-O-O 15 Q×BP R-N5 16 P-KN3 P-B4 17 N-B5! N-Q2 18 N×B+ Q×N 19 Q×BP R×QP 20 Q×KP Q-B1 21 B-KB4 R×B.B5 22 P×R Q×P+ 23 K-N1 1-0.

Other sixth moves are just as bad for Black. e.g.

a) 6...B-Q2 7 B-K2 B-B3 8 O-O R-N1 9 P-B4 B-Q3 10 Q-B2 P-B4? 11 P-Q5!±;

b) 6...P-QB4 7 B-K3 Q-N3 8 B-K2 N-B3 9 O-O B-Q2 (not 9...P×P? 10 N×P B-B4 11 P-QB3 P-K4 12 N-N5! B×B 13 Q-Q6! winning) 10 P-B3 B-K2 11 P-Q5! and Black's pawns will be seriously weakened, Richter-Petrov, 1936; or

c) 6...B-Q3 7 B-Q3 P-N3 8 B-K4 P-B3 9 O-O B-N2 10 B-K3 P-KB4 11 B-Q3+.

7 B-QN5+!	P-B3
8 B-QB4	B-QN2

If 8...B-QR3 9 B×B N×B 10 P-B3± (Black's knight is poorly placed), or if 8...Q-B2 9 O-O B-QN2 10 R-K1 N-Q2 (not 10...B-K2? 11 Q-K2 N-Q2 12 B×P! P×B 13 Q×P N×B1 14 Q×KBP N-N3 14 B-N5 winning, Tokarev-Makarov, USSR 1951) 11 Q-K2± — B×P is again threatened and the black king would not be happy after Q-side castling either.

9 B-B4	B-Q3
10 B-KN3	Q-B2
11 Q-K2	N-Q2
12 O-O	O-O-O
13 B-R6±	

This position was reached in the game Liublinsky-Ufimsev, USSR Championship Semi-Final 1945. White's advantage lies principally in the fact that his king is much less vulnerable than Black's, the black pawns at QB3 and QN3 providing White with targets for his Q-side pawns to attack.

The game continued: 13...P-R4 14 B×B+ K×B 15 P-B4 ±

B4

1 P-K4 P-QB3 2 P-Q4 P-Q4 3 P×P P×P 4 P-QB4 N-KB3 5 P-B5

4 ...	N-Q2(*46*)

The normal move, preparing to play ...KN-B3 under the best possible circumstances.

5 N-KB3	KN-B3

5...B-K2 6 B-Q3 KN-B3 7 N×N+ transposes to the text after

46

7...N×N. If instead Black tries 7...B×N, White can obtain good attacking chances with Pachman's suggestion 8 Q-K2 O-O 9 B-K3 R-K1 10 O-O-O P-B4 11 P-KR4.

      6 N×N+   N×N
      7 B-Q3

We have reached an important position in the Rubinstein Variation. White's plan is to increase his hold on the centre by Q-Q2 and B-KN5, and then continue with either O-O followed by R-Q1 or O-O-O followed by P-KR4.

Black has tried various moves from this position and we examine the more plausible of them under:

B41 7...P-QB4
B42 7...B-K2
B43 7...P-QN3

7...P-KR3 prevents one of White's key moves but in doing so it wastes a tempo and creates a weakness. Spielmann-L'Hermet, 1927 continued: 8 Q-K2 B-Q3 9 B-Q2 O-O 10 O-O-O B-Q2 11 N-K5 P-B4 12 P×P B×N 13 Q×B B-B3 14 B-KB4± with excellent attacking chances.

7...P-B3 is also weak. Prins-Guimard, 1950 continued: 8 B-K3 B-K2 9 Q-K2 Q-R4+ 10 B-Q2 Q-B2 11 O-O-O N-Q4 12 N-K5 B-B3 13 P-KB4 P-QN4 14 KR-B1 P-QR3 15 B-K4 R-R2 16 R-B3± (space advantage and extra mobility). Black's KR is useless because . . .O-O would result in him getting mated.

B41

1 P-K4 P-K3 2 P-Q4 P-Q4 3 N-QB3 P×P 4 N×P N-Q2 5 N-KB3 KN-B3 6 N×N+ N×N 7 B-Q3

      7 ...   P-QB4(*47*)

      8 P×P   B×P

If 8...Q-R4+ 9 B-Q2 Q×BP, 10 Q-K2 followed by O-O-O gives White a clear advantage due to three distinct factors: (1) He has a two move

lead in development; (2) He has a Q-side pawn majority; (3) He has good prospects of an attack against Black's K-side.

    9 B-KN5

Threatening 10 B×N Q×B 11 B-N5+.

    9 ...   B-K2

9...O-O 10 Q-K2 P-KR3 11 B-Q2! followed by O-O-O produces a position of the kind discussed earlier (±).

    If 9...B-Q2 10 Q-K2 Q-B2 11 O-O O-O-O 12 N-K5±

    10   Q-K2   O-O
    11   O-O-O

White has completed his development and is now ready to launch a K-side attack. Spielmann-Petrov, 1938.

B42

    1 P-K4 P-K3 2 P-Q4 P-Q4 3 N-QB3 P×P 4 N×P N-Q2 5 N-KB3 KN-B3 6 N×N+ N×N 7 B-Q3

    7 ...   B-K2(*48*)

    8 B-KN5

The most aggressive move.

    8 ...   P-B4

After 8...P-KR3, Keres recommends simply 9 B-R4.

8...N-Q4 is a rather surprising move that fails to accomplish anything. Ljubisavljevic-Canal, San Benedetto 1967, continued 9 B×B Q×B 10 O-O O-O 11 R-K1 N-B5 12 B-K4 R-Q1 13 Q-Q2 Q-Q3 14 QR-Q1 N-Q4 15 N-K5 N-B3 16 B-Q3± — White's superior development gives him greater freedom of action.

Black's only serious alternative to the text is 8...O-O 9 Q-K2 and now;

a) 9...P-B4 10 O-O-O P×P 11 P-KR4 is good for White (Tal);

b) 9...Q-Q4 10 O-O P-KR3 11 P-B4 Q-Q3 12 B-R4 shows Black's early queen excursion to be mere loss of time, Matulovic-Canal, Reggio Emilia 1968-69; or

c) 9...R-N1 10 O-O-O P-QN3 11 KR-K1 B-N2 (so far as in Pantaleev-Popov, Bulgaria 1967) 12 N-K5± — White has a fine centralized position and Black's king will be in permanent danger.

9	Q-K2	P×P
10	O-O-O	P-QR3

If 10...O-O, 11 P-KR4 is strong (as is mentioned before).

11	KR-K1	B-Q2

If 11...O-O then 12 K-N1! followed by N×P, or 11...N-Q4 12 B×B Q×B 13 Q-K5!, when 13...O-O is not possible because of 14 Q×N winning a piece.

12	N×P	Q-R4
13	N-B5	P-KR3

Not 13...Q×P 14 N×P+ K-B1 15 B-R6!

14	N×P+	K-B1
15	B×N	B×B
16	B-B4!	

Simultaneously defending the QRP and attacking the bishop at Q7.

16	...	Q-KN4+
17	K-N1	B-N4
18	B×B	Q×N
19	B-R4!	

Black is completely lost. His king is awkwardly placed, his rooks both undeveloped and his queen and bishop doing nothing of any consequence. Tal-Barcza, 1962 concluded: 19...P-N4 (if 19...B×P 20 Q-K4 B-R6 21 Q×NP±±) 20 B-N3 B×P 21 Q-K4 R-K1 (or 21...R-B1 22 Q-QN4+ K-N1 23 B×P! B-B6 24 B×P+ winning) 22 Q-N4+ K-N1 23 R-K3 K-R2 24 R-N3 Q-K4 25 P-KB4 Q-K7 26 K×B! P-QR4 (26...Q×R 27 Q-K4+ P-B4 28 Q-N7+ etc.) 27 R-Q7! 1-0.

B43

1 P-K4 P-K3 2 P-Q4 P-Q4 3 NpQB3 P×P 4 N×P N-Q2 5 N-KB3 KN-B3 6 N×N+ N×N 7 B-Q3

7 ...   P-QN3(*49*)

8 Q-K2

With the same plan as before (see B42).

8 ...		B-N2
9	B-KN5	B-K2
10	O-O-O	O-O

If 10...Q-Q4 11 K-N1±

| 11 | P-KR4 | Q-Q4 |

Not 11...P-B4 12 K-N1 Q-B2 13 R-R3 KR-Q1 14 R-K1 QR-B1 15 N-K5± Milner Barry — Wade, Nottingham 1946.

12	K-N1	KR-Q1
13	P-B4	Q-Q3
14	KR-K1	P-KR3
15	B-B1	B-KB1
16	N-K5±	

Bronstein-Kan, Moscow Championship 1947.

B5 Other fourth moves

After 1 P-K4 P-K3 2 P-Q4 P-Q4 3 N-QB3 P×P 4 N×P, there are four other moves to which I should give a brief mention.

a) 4...N-QB3 5 N-KB3 B-K2 6 P-B3 N-B3 7 B-Q3 O-O 8 Q-B2 P-KR3 9 B-Q2 P-QN3 10 O-O-O B-N2 11 N×N+ B×N 12 KR-K1 N-K2 13 N-K5± Black's castled position is somewhat vulnerable because of the weakening . . .P-KR3;

b) 4...P-QN3 5 Q-B3 P-QB3 6 B-KN5!±;

c) 4...P-K4? 5 N-KB3 B-KN5 6 B-QB4 (threatening 7 B×P+ K×B 8 N×P+ K moves 9 N×B±±) 6...P-KB3 7 O-O±; Black's loss of two tempi gives him a poor game;

d) 4...Q-Q4 5 Q-B3 Q×QP 6 N-K2 with ample compensation for the sacrificed pawn.

C

1 P-K4 P-K3 2 P-Q4 P-Q4 3 N-QB3

3 ... N-KB3(*50*)

50

4 P-K5

An old idea originally popularized by Steinitz.

4 ... N3-Q2

4...N-K5 lands Black in difficulties at once because after 5 N×N P×N 6 B-K3, his advanced KP becomes a distinct liability. e.g. 6...P-QB4 7 P×P N-Q2 8 Q-N4±. Troianescu-Wade, Bucharest 1954, now continued: 8...P-B4? (better would have been 8...N×KP 9 Q×P.K4±) 9 P×Pep N×KBP 10 B-QN5+ K-B2 11 Q-K2 Q-B2 12 N-R3 B×P (better is 12...P-KR3) 13 N-N5+ K-K2 14 Q-B4!±

4...N-N1 is not quite so ridiculous as might first appear. The idea is to take advantage of White's advance P-K5 by manoeuvering the KN to ...KB4. As a suitable counter to this paln I suggest 5 N3-K2 so that 5...P-QB4 can be met by 6 P-QB3, and 5...N-K2 by 6 N-N3 (preventing both ...N-B4 and ...P-KR4) followed by Q-N4.

5 N3-K2

The idea of this move is clear. White intends to bolster his central pawns by P-QB3 followed by P-KB4 and then to play for the advance P-KB5. The system has only been seen sporadically in master chess but it was given a new lease of life by the Danish International Master Enevoldsen who played it frequently during the early 1950s. For our main line we follow the game Kavalek-Marovic, Amsterdam 1968.

5 ...	P-QB4
6 P-B3	N-QB3

6...P-B3 weakens Black's KP and it is therefore not surprising that Euwe suggests 7 N-B4! as White's strongest counter. e.g. 7...Q-K2 8 B-Q3 Q-B2 9 N-B3 and Black must retreat a knight to the back rank.

7 P-B4	Q-N3

Alternatives are:

a) 7...P-QN4!? is an interesting idea of Lasker's designed to increase Black's Q-side space before continuing his pressure on White's QP with ...Q-N3. After 8 N-B3 P-N5!? (not 8...Q-N3 9 P-QR3 P-QR4 10 P-B5 BP×P 11 KBP×P BP×P 12 P×P B-K2 13 N-B4± Enevoldsen-Czerniak, Helsinki 1952) White does best to play 9 P-KN3 with the idea of B-R3 followed by O-O and P-B5 (±).

b) 7...P×P 8 P×P B-N5+ (or 8...Q-R4+ 9 B-Q2 Q-N3 10 B-B3±) 9 B-Q2 Q-N3 10 N-KB3 O-O 11 B×B Q×B+12 Q-Q2± Tarrasch-Noa, 1885. Black's bishop is very 'bad', his king is unfavourably placed for the endgame and White has a space advantage to boot.

c) 7...B-K2 8 N-B3 O-O 9 P-KN3 P×P (or 9...P-B4 10 P×Pep N×BP 11 B-N2 P×P 12 N2×P N×N 13 P×N N-K5 14 O-O and again Black's QB is severely restricted, Enevoldsen-Teschner, Helsinki 1952) 10 P×P N-N3 11 N-B3! followed by B-Q3, O-O, Q-K2 and B-K3 with advantage to White — Alekhine.

d) 7...P-B3 8 N-B3 P-QN4 is a suggestion of Pachman's. The idea is to continue with ...Q-N3, ...P-B4 (to blockade the centre) and play on the Q-side. As an interesting and virile counter to this plan I suggest 9 P-B5! e.g. 9...KP×P 10 N-B4! (threatening the QNP as well as the QP); or 9...KBP×P 10 BP×P followed by 11 P×KP and 12 N-B4.

7...P-B3 8 N-B3 Q-N3 transposes to the text.

8 N-B3	P-B3
9 P-KN3	QBP×P
10 BP×P	B-N5+

10...P×P 11 BP×P B-N5+ is less flexible than the text: 12 N-B3 O-O (threatening 13...R×N 14 Q×R N×QP and 15...N×KP) 13 B-KB4 B-K2 14 P-QR3! P-KN4 (not 14...Q×NP? 15 N-QR4 winning the queen, not 14...R-B2? (too defensive) 15 N-QR4 Q-Q1 16 P-R4 N-B1 17 B-Q3 B-Q2 18 P-QN4 P-QN3 19 N-B3 P-QR4 20 P-N5 N-R2 21 N-KN5! with an overwhelming game for White, Dubinin-Alatortsev, USSR 1947) 15 N-QR4 Q-Q1 16 B-K3± Black has weakened his castled position and White even has the better game on the Q-side — traditionally Black's preserve in the French.

11 B-Q2!	

This important innovation is Kavalek's improvement on the accepted response 11 N-B3. His idea is to exchange off White's 'bad' bishop for Black's 'good' one.

11	...	B×B+
12	Q×B	O-O
13	B-N2	

Ivkov suggests 13 B-R3 as a possible alternative.

13	...	P-QR4
14	O-O	P-R5
15	K-R1	N-R4
16	Q-B3!	

Forestalling Black's . . .N-B5.

16	...	Q-N4
17	R-B2	R-R3
18	Q-B2	N-B5
19	N-B3	Q-R4

19...N-K6? helps White considerably. After 20 Q-K2 Q×Q 21 R×Q N×B 22 K×N, White threatens 23 P-B5! and 22... P-B4 can be met by 23 N-QN5!

20	R-K1	P×P
21	BP×P±	

The Kavalek-Marovic game concluded: 21...Q-Q1 22 P-R4 P-R3 23 P-N3 P×P 24 P×P N-R4 25 N-QN5 R-QB3 26 Q-Q3 P-QN3! 27 N-R3 R-KB2 28 B-B1 Q-B1 29 N-QN5?! B-R3 30 Q-K3 B×N 31 B×B R-B2 32 R1-KB1 Q-N5?? (the best way to meet White's threatened 33 N-N5! R×R 34 R×R was 32...Q-K2 when Ivkov assesses the position as unclear. Possibly White can then afford to play 33 P-KN4!? with the idea of P-N5, e.g. 33...R×N 34 Q×R Q×P+ 35 K-N1 Q-K2 36 Q-B7+ Q×Q 37 R×Q and White wins a piece.) 33 N-N5 R×R 34 Q×R 1-0.

8 Caro-Kann Defence

1 P-K4 P-QB3

This closed defence is endowed with a reputation of solid dependability which has been built up partly by the results of such defensive maestros as Capablanca and Botvinnik. Many tactical players cringe with horror at the sight of Black's first move 1...P-QB3. 'How dull' they say to themselves. 'Why doesn't he take up fishing instead of chess?'

It is true that the Caro-Kann offers White little or no scope (in the main lines) of reaching the type of position in which a tactician can revel. The reader might therefore be thankful to receive a little known weapon which *DOES* create sharp positions against the Caro-Kann, almost by force. This weapon was first suggested in 1951 by the German analyst Gerhart Gunderam and apart from an extensive analysis in his book *Neue Eröffnungswege* it is hardly mentioned in chess literature.

1 P-K4	P-QB3
2 P-Q4	P-Q4
3 P×P	P×P
4 P-QB4	N-KB3

4...N-QB3 is met by 5P×P! Q×P 6 N-KB3, when a position is reached that can also arise out of our recommended system against the Sicilian Defence: 1 P-K4 P-QB4 2 P-QB3 P-Q4 3 P×P Q×P 4 P-Q4 P×P?! 5 P×P N-QB3 6 N-KB3. For further analysis of this variation the reader is referred to page XX.

5 P-B5 (*51*)

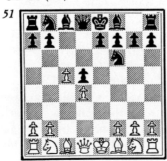

This move initiates the Gunderam Attack. The basis of White's system is the immediate utilization of his Q-side pawn majority which, if allowed too much leeway, will soon result in the creation of at least one and often two passed pawns wreaking havoc amongst Black's Q-side army.

The analysis which follows is due, almost in its entirety to Gunderam. He considers:

A 5...P-QN3
B 5...P-K4
C 5...P-QR4
D 5...P-K3
E 5...Q-B2
F 5...P-KN3
G 5...N-B3

A

1 P-K4 P-QB3 2 P-Q4 P-Q4 3 P×P P×P 4 P-QB4 N-KB3 5 P-B5

        5 ...   P-QN3

This and 5...P-K4 possibly represent Black's most logical attempts since they are the only moves that confer an immediate attack on White's pawn chain.

        6 P-QN4   P-QR4

Also:

a) A different move which also accomplishes this task is 6...P-K4, but then 7 QP×P N-K5 (7...N3-Q2 8 Q×P leaves Black devoid of compensation after 8...Q-K2 9 P-B4 or 8...Q-B2 9 P-B4, while 7...N-N5 is refuted even more drastically by 8 B-QN5+ B-Q2 9 P-B6! because on 9...B×NP+ 10 B-Q2 Black must lose a piece.) 8 B-QN5+ B-Q2 9 Q×P presents White with a winning material advantage: 9...B×B 10 Q×R B-B3 11 Q×P and:

a1) 11...N-B6 12 N×N B×NP fails to 13 B-N5 N-B3 (otherwise 14 R-Q1 will be killing) 14 B×Q N×Q 15 B×P leaves White a rook and three pawns ahead with no real obstacle in his way. After 15...N-B1 16 KN-K2 B×R (16...N×B 17 R-KN1) 17 O-O-O, Black can resign with confidence.

a2) 11...P×P 12 B-K3 and at the correct moment White's P-B3 will bring about the total collapse of Black's game.

b) 6...P-K3 is too slow and after 7 B-N2 followed by P-QR3, White's pawn majority will prove too much for Black to handle. In fact the only master game that has tested the Gunderam Attack reached this line, but no real conclusion can be drawn from the game because White played all his moves in 15 minutes and rushed off for a date with a local wench: 7 B-K3 P×P 8 QP×P P-QR4 9 Q-R4+ N3-Q2 10 N-Q2 B-N2 11

N-N3 P×P 12 Q×P Q-B2 13 N-B3 P-K4 14 B-QN5 N-QB3 15 B×N B×B
16 O-O R-R5 17 Q-B3 B-K2 18 KR-K1 O-O 19 Q-N2 R-N1 20 B-Q4 P-
B3 21 Q-K2 B-B1 22 QR-B1 K-R1 23 B-R1 Q-R2 24 N.B3-Q4 P×N 25
N×P N-K4 26 Q×N P×Q 27 N×B Q-QB2 28 N×R P-K5 29 P-B6 Q×N 30
P-B7 Q-B1 31 B-K5 P-R3 32 R-N1 R-B5 33 R-N8 Q-K3 34 R×B+ K-R2
35 B-B4 P-Q5 36 P-KR3 P-K6 37 P×P P-N4 38 B-K5 P-Q6 39 R1-KB1
Q×B 40 P-B8=Q Q×P+ 41 K-R1 R×Q 42 R×R Q-K7 43 R-KB7+ K-N3
44 R-Q7 Q×RP 45 R8-Q8 $^1_2$-$^1_2$, Mariotti-Flesch, Sombor 1970.
    c) 6...P×P 7 QP×P! P-K3 8 B-N2 has a similar effect e.g. 8...P-QR4 9
Q-R4+ B-Q2 10 B-N5 N-R3 11 P-QR3± or 8...B-Q2 (or 8...N-B3) 9 N-
KB3 with a firm grip on the centre as well as a Q-side plus.
    Now back to the main line.

                    7 P-N5

Already the pawn majority is beginning to roll.

            7 ...   P×P
            8 P×P   Q-B2
    On 8...P-K4 9 P-B6 or 8...QN-Q2 9 P-B6 followed by Q-Q4, the
situation on the Q-side has fully justified Gunderam's 5 P-B5.

                    9 B-K3

Now White's passed pawns are both protected and Black is probably
already helpless against their combined force.

            9 ...   QN-Q2

    If 9...N-N5 10 P-B6! and Black's QN is entombed, while 9...P-K4 10
Q-R4 B-Q2 11 P-N6 has an even more disastrous effect on Black's
game.
            10   P-N6   Q-K4

    10...Q-N2 is refuted by 11 B-QN5 (with obvious continuation) and
10...Q-B3 by 11 P-QR4 or 11 N-QB3 to be followed by B-QN5 and P-
B6.
            11   N-Q2   N×BP
            12   R-B1!(52)

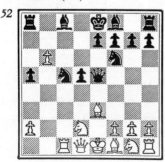

Continuing in the spirit of the variation, White has developed his Q-side while leaving the other wing untouched and even at this early stage in the game Gunderam's analysis suggests that Black is lost in all variations:

a) 12...P-K3 13 KN-B3 winning a piece;

b) 12...N3-K5 13 N×N N×N 14 B-QN5+ B-Q2 15 P-N7 R-Q1 (if 15...R-QN1 16 R-B8+!!) 16 B×B+ R×B 17 R-B8+ R-Q1 18 Q-R4 mate;

c) 12...N4-K5 13 B-QN5+ B-Q2 14 P-N7 R-Q1 15 R-B8 B×B 16 Q-N3 P-Q5 17 B×P N×N+ 18 B×Q N×Q 19 R×R+ etc.;

d) 12...N3-Q2 13 B-QN5 P-K3 14 KN-B3 Q-N7 15 P-QR4 Q-N5 (15...N-N2 16 B-Q4) 16 N-K5 and the threat of 17 P-N7 leaves Black helpless;

e) 12...N-N2 13 B-QR6 N-Q3 (or 13...Q-N1 14 B-QN5+ B-Q2 15 Q-R4 N-Q3 16 B×B+ N×B 17 R-B7 Q-Q1 18 KN-B3 when Black cannot prevent this knight from coming to K5 or Q4, winning instantly.) 14 R×B+ R×R 15 B×R N×B 16 P-N7 N-R2 17 KN-B3 Q-N1 18 B×N Q×B 19 Q-R4+ K-Q1 (19...N-Q2 20 Q-B6) 20 N-K5 etc.;

f) 12...N4-Q2 13 Q-N3 Q-N1 14 R-B7 B-N2 15 B-QN5 P-K4 16 B×N+ N×B 17 Q-N5 B-B1 18 N-K2 with the powerful threat of R×B+ followed by P-N7.

In each of the above variations Black has lost because of the vulnerability of his Q-side and the strength of White's advanced QNP. This whole line serves to highlight many of the tactical resources that White has at his disposal in the Gunderam Attack.

B

1 P-K4 P-QB3 2 P-Q4 P-Q4 3 P×P P×P 4 P-QB4 N-KB3 5 P-B5

5 ...   P-K4(*53*)

53
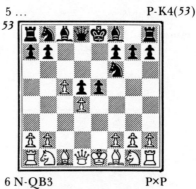

6 N-QB3   P×P

On 6...P-K5? 7 P-QN4, the blockade in the centre deprives Black of any counterplay there and White's pawn majority has a free hand as it rolls towards the far side of the board.

7 Q×P   B-K2

7...N-B3 at once is met by the awkward stroke 8 B-QN5 B-Q2 9 B×N! e.g. 9...B×B 10 P-QN4 P-QR3 11 KN-K2 P-KN3 12 B-N2 B-N2 13 R-Q1 O-O 14 O-O N-K5 15 Q-Q3, and if now 15...P-B4 then 16 N-Q4 followed by an eventual P-B3. 9...P×B 10 KN-K2 also gives Black problems. e.g. 10...P-N3 11 B-B4! and Black's QB is a 'bad' piece or 10...Q-K2 11 N-R4 N-K5 12 P-QN4 P-QR4 13 P-QR3 P×P 14 P×P followed by B-N2 and White will eventually reach a 'good' knight v 'bad' bishop ending.

8 B-K3	O-O
9 R-Q1	N-B3
10 Q-QR4	

Black has no compensation for either his isolated QP or White's mobile Q-side majority. White can complete his development with ease and after 10...R-K1 11 B-K2 or 10...B-K3 11 N-B3 he enjoys a distinct advantage in an open position.

C

1 P-K4 P-QB3 2 P-Q4 P-Q4 3 P×P P×P 4 P-QB4 N-KB3 5 P-B5

5 ...	P-QR4(*54*)

Preventing 6 P-QN4.

54

6 N-QB3	P-QN3

6...P-K4 7 P×P is at least as good for White as in the similar positions already examined. e.g. 7...N3-Q2 8 Q×P B×P 9 N-B3 followed by B-Q3 and O-O, when Black has nothing to show for his pawn minus, or 7...N-N5 8 B-QN5+ N-B3 9 P-KR3 N×BP (or 9...N×KP 10 Q×P) 10 K×N B×BP+ 11 K-B1 Q-R5 12 Q-K1! and White wins.

7 N-R4!	P×P
8 P×P	P-K3
9 P-QR3	B-Q2

9...N-K5 10 P-QN4 Q-B3 fails to 11 B-QN5+ B-Q2 12 B×B+ N×B 13 B-K3 N-K4 14 R-B1! N-B5 15 N-QB3, when Black will have no adequate means of preventing the eventual advance of White's Q-side majority.

10	P-QN4	P×P
11	P×P	N-B3
12	B-R3	R×N

Otherwise 13 N-N6 will be too strong since it enables White to exchange on Q7 at will and he can choose the moment in such a way as to maximize the effect of the follow-up P-N5 and P-B6.

13	Q×R	N-K5

Threatening 14...N×KBP 15 K×N Q-B3+.

14	R-B1	Q-B3

If 14...N-Q5 15 P-N5 Q-B3 16 Q-R8+ Q-Q1 17 Q×Q+ K×Q 18 P-N6. White, the exchange ahead and still with his united passed pawns, has a clearly won game.

15	N-B3	N-Q5
16	P-N5!	N×N+
17	P×N	

and Black can resign after 17...N-N4 18 B-K2.

D

1 P-K4 P-QB3 2 P-Q4 P-Q4 3 P×P P×P 4 P-QB4 N-KB3 5 P-B5

5 ...	P-K3 (55)

A passive move which fails to contest White's Q-side advances.

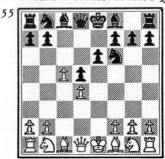

6	P-QN4	P-QR4
7	P-N5	P-K4

So Black has already conceded a tempo.

8	N-QB3	P×P
9	Q×P	Q-K2+

9...Q-B2 10 N-R4 N-K5 11 B-K3 (followed by R-B1) leaves White's passed pawns strongly supported.

10	B-K3	B-K3

11   P-B3

White's king will be safe on KB2, and N-R4 followed by R-B1 will lead to a position similar to that arising in the last note. The advanced white pawns at QN5 and QB5 once again dominate the proceedings.

E

1 P-K4 P-QB3 2 P-Q4 P-Q4 3 PxP PxP 4 P-QB4 N-KB3 5 P-B5

5 ...   Q-B2(*56*)

6 N-QB3!   P-QR3

Black must protect his QN4 square e.g. 6...P-K4 7 N-N5 Q-Q1 8 PxP N-K5 9 N-Q6+ BxN 10 BPxB±; or 6...B-Q2 7 N-B3 N-B3 8 B-QN5! and if 8...P-QR3 then 9 BxN PxB 10 N-K5 followed by B-B4 when White's advantage will lie in the 'good' knight v 'bad' bishop ending. (Compare variation B, note to Black's seventh move).

The disadvantages of the text move are that it does nothing to advance Black's development and it contributes significantly to the weakening of the dark squares.

7 Q-B3   Q-B3

7...B-N5? and 7...N-B3? both lose a pawn to 8 NxP while 7...P-K3 8 B-KB4 gives White a positional plus because of his extra Q-side space and his control of the dark squares.

8 P-QN4   B-N5

Not 8 ...P-K4 9 P-N5.

9 Q-N3   Q-B1

If 9...Q-K3+ 10 Q-K5, followed by QxQ. P-QR4, B-N2 and P-N5±. The point of the text move is that it overprotects the QB. Another move that serves this aim is 9...P-KR4, but after 10 P-KR3 B-B4 11 B-KB4 White has complete control of the dark squares.

10   P-KR3   B-B4
11   P-R3

This position is typical of the whole variation, White proceeding calmly with B-N2, N-B3 and an eventual P-QR4 and P-N5. This plan, aided by White's control of the dark squares, guarantees the first player a lasting advantage.

F

1 P-K4 P-QB3 2 P-Q4 P-Q4 3 P×P P×P 4 P-QB4 N-KB3 5 P-B5

      5 ...   P-KN3(*57*)

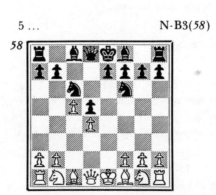

An insipid move that does nothing to oppose White's strategy.

6 B-K3	B-N2
7 N-QB3	O-O
8 N-B3	B-N5
9 B-K2	B×N
10 B×B	N-B3
11 P-QR3	P-QR4
12 R-QN1	R-K1
13 O-O	

Once again Black can offer little resistance to White's Q-side advance. After P-QN4 P×P, P×P followed by Q-N3 and R-R1, White has the traditional advantage of the advanced pawn majority.

G

      5 ...   N-B3(*58*)

6 B-QN5	P-QR4

Essential so as to prevent 7 P-QN4. If instead Black tries the usual central counter-stroke 6...P-K4, the result is a position akin to those in variation B (note to Black's seventh move) and variation E (note to Black's sixth): 7 N-KB3 P×P 8 Q×P N-K5 9 P-QN4 B-K2 10 B-KB4 O-O 11 B×N P×B 12 O-O B-R3 13 R-K1 B-B3 14 B-K5. The black pawns at QB3 and Q4 form an inherently weak structure which provides White with the strong squares Q4 and K5 for use by his knights.

7 P-QR3	P-K4
8 N-KB3	P×P
9 Q×P	B-Q2
10 B×N	B×B

10...P×B leads to the type of position mentioned in the previous note.

11 O-O	N-K5
12 P-QN4	B-K2
13 Q-N2!	B-B3
14 N-Q4	

Black has run out of play and White is free to complete his development by B-K3 and N-Q2.

Conclusion: Gunderam's Attack is an unusually virile counter to the Caro-Kann Defence. It at once provides White with a strong pawn in the enemy camp and offers him various possibilities based on the support of this pawn by P-QN4 and the eventual advance of either or both of the pair. Since Gunderam's analysis is almost completely untested, the reader has ample opportunity for original creative work within this system.

9 Alekhine's Defence

1 P-K4 N-KB3

Up to the mid 1950s the most popular counter to Alekhine's Defence was the Four Pawns Attack. While builds up an imposing pawn centre with pawns at QB4, Q4 and K5, and in conjunction with classical piece development (knights at KB3 and QB3 and bishops at K3 and K2) his position has all the appearance of being a dominating one. After many years of master experience with the Four Pawns Attack it was discovered that Black has, in the crucial position, perfectly adequate counterplay based on the move . . .P-KB3 followed by a strike at the centre with an eventual . . .P-K4.

Because of this opinion, masters facing Alekhine's Defence turned away from the Four Pawns and expressed a preference for quieter systems that were typified by the move 4 N-KB3. Now, because of a game won by the brilliant Yugoslav grandmaster Velimirovic, the Four Pawns Attack is back in vogue. The reason is that Velimirovic has revived a line in which White forsakes castling, avoids the crucial position mentioned above, and instead proceeds with an early central attack heralded by the thrust P-Q5.

2 P-K5	N-Q4

After 2...N-K5? 3 P-Q3 N-B4 4 P-Q4 White enjoys a great advantage in space. e.g. 4...N-K3 5 P-Q5± or 4...N4-R3 5 P-KB4±. If 2...N-N1 3 P-Q4 P-Q4 (or 3...P-Q3 4 P×P) 4 P×Pep KP×P 5 B-Q3 N-QB3 6 N-K2 N-B3 7 B-KN5 B-K2 8 Q-Q2±, Vesely-Alster, Czechoslovakia 1961, Black's passive play has resulted in White having much greater freedom of movement.

3 P-QB4	N-N3
4 P-Q4	P-Q3

4...N-B3?? loses a piece to 5 P-Q5. e.g.

a) 5...N×KP 6 P-B5 N3-B5 7 P-B4;

b) 5...N-N5 6 P-B5 N3×P 7 P-QR3; or

c) 5...N-N1 6 P-B5.

4...P-Q4? allows White to obtain an enormous advantage in space by

5 P-B5 N3-Q2 6 P-QN4 P-QN3 7 P-QR3.

     5 P-B4(*59*)

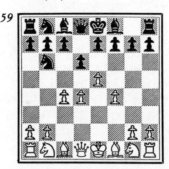

This position marks the start of the Four Pawns Attack. Black has encouraged White to create this particular pawn formation in the hope that (1) it will soon provide a target for Black's counter-attack, and (2) the vacum created behind White's pawn mass will eventually give Black a hunting ground for his pieces.

     5 ...   P×P

Inferior alternatives are:

a) 5...P-KN4?! The purpose of this outlandish thrust is to lure one of White's pawns away from the centre but it would seem that Black has great difficulty in justifying his sacrifice of a pawn. The game Tringov-Planinc, Varna 1970, continued: 6 KP×P NP×P (on 6...Q×P 7 P-B5 Q-K3+ 8 K-B2! N-Q4 9 P×P, Black again lacks anything to show for his pawn) 7 P×BP Q×BP 8 N-QB3 P-K4 9 P×P N-B3 10 B×P B-K3 11 N-K4 B-QN5+ 12 K-B2 N×BP 13 B×N B×B 14 N-KB3 R-Q1 15 Q-QB1 Q-N3+ 16 B-K3, and White had no difficulty in maintaining his advantage.

b) 5...B-B4?! The idea behind this move is that Black hopes for the continuation 6 N-QB3 P×P 7 BP×P P-K3 8 B-K3 B-QN5, when the variation discussed on page XX (note to Black's 6th move) has been reached. The fault in this transposition lies in the fact that White can safely play the immediate B-Q3! without having to worry about ...N×QP. After 5...B-B4?! 6 B-Q3! B×B 7 Q×B P×P 8 BP×P, White's pawn mass does not suffer from the same vulnerability of some other lines and his advantage in space guarantees him a clear plus. e.g. 8...N-B3 9 N-KB3 P-K3 10 P-QR3 Q-Q2 11 P-QN4! R-Q1 12 B-K3, Euwe-Colle, Brussels 1927; or 8...P-QB4 9 N-KB3 P-K3 10 O-O N-B3 11 N-B3 N×QP 12 B-N5! Q-Q2 13 N-K4 P-KR3 14 B-B6! with a strong attack. Platonov-Kupreichik, USSR 1966, continued: 14...Q-B3 15 B×P B×B 16 N-Q6+ K-B1 17 N×N P×N 18 R×P+ K-N1 19 Q-N6 R-R2

20 R1-KB1 K-R1 21 R-K7 N×P 22 N-B7+ and White was winning.

c) 5...P-KN3 is unthematic and permits White to transpose to a superior form of the Pirc Defence: 6 B-K3 B-N2 7 N-QB3 O-O (7...P×P 8 BP×P P-QB4 9 P×P N3-Q2 10 P-K6 P×P 11 N-B3 Q-R4 12 R-B1 N×P 13 B-Q4 is somewhat better for White. Samisch-Rellstab, Germany 1931) 8 N-B3 P×P (8...B-N5 9 P-QB5! and 8...B-K3 9 P-QN3! both augment White's advantage) 9 QP×P! Experience has shown that White enjoys a slight advantage in this position. e.g. 9...N-B3 10 P-QB5 N-Q2 11 B-B4 P-K3 12 O-O P-N3 13 Q-R4 B-N2 14 B-N5, Kupper-Schmid, Zurich 1956; or 9...P-QB3 10 Q-N3 B-N5 11 B-K2 B×N 12 B×B Q-Q6 13 N-K4 Q×Q 14 P×Q, Matanovic-Darga, Bordeaux 1964.

6 BP×P   N-B3

6...P-QB4 is a very trappy move designed to undermine the support of White's KP. White should continue: 7 P-Q5 P-K3 (not 7...B-B4 8 N-QB3 P-K3 9 B-K2 N-R3 10 P-QR3 P×P 11 P×P N-B2, because of 12 P-Q6 N-K3 13 B-QN5+ N-Q2 14 N-B3 P-QR3 15 B×N+ Q×B 16 O-O O-O-O 17 N-Q5 Q-B3 18 N-N5! winning the exchange and the game.) 8 N-QB3 P×P (8...Q-R5+ 9 P-KN3 Q-Q5 is best met by 10 B-Q2! Q×KP+ 11 B-K2 P×P 12 N-B3 and if 12...Q-K3 13 O-O B-K2 14 R-K1 O-O 15 P×P, or 12...Q-Q3 13 B-B4 Q-Q1 14 O-O with advantage to White in both cases because of his substantial lead in development.) 9 P×P Q-R5+ (9...P-B5! can be answered by Bagirov's interesting suggestion 10 P-Q6! with the idea of N-B3 followed by B-KN5 as one possibility, and N-QN5 as another.) 10 P-KN3 Q-Q5 11 B-QN5+! B-Q2 12 Q-K2, and White's advantage is probably decisive. e.g.

a) 12... P-QR3 13 P-K6! P×P 14 Q×P+ B-K2 15 B-N5 N-B1 16 B.QN5×B or

b) 12...N×P 13 P-K6! P×P (or 13...B×B 14 N×B Q-QN5+ 15 B-Q2 Q×P 16 P×P++ K×P 17 Q-R5+ K-K3 18 N-KB3! Q×R+ 19 K-B2! winning) 14 Q×P+ N-K2 15 N-B3 Q-B3 16 Q-K2 B×B 17 N×B N-R3 18 B-N5 Q-QN3 19 O-O-O R-Q1 20 R×R+ K×R 21 R-Q1+ K-B1 22 B-B4 1-0. Balashov-K. Grigorian, Riga 1967.

6...B-B4 7 N-QB3 P-K3 8 N-B3 B-QN5 is an idea that has enjoyed some popularity recently. It avoids the main line and contains some unpleasant surprises for White if he is not careful. But with 9 B-Q3! White retains the initiative. Velimirovic-Martz, Vrnjacka Banja 1973, continued 9...B-N5 (on 9...B×B 10 Q×B P-QB4 11 O-O White threatens 12 N-K4) 10 O-O N-B3 (10...B.KN5×N? 11 Q×B Q×P+ 12 B-K3 Q-Q2 13 QR-Q1 is fatal for Black) 11 P-B5! B.QN5×N 12 P×B N-Q4 13 Q-K1! N4-K2 14 R-N1 R-QN1 15 N-N5±—Black's monarch must face the combined onslaught of all White's pieces.

7 B-K3	B-B4
8 N-QB3	P-K3

If Black tries to undermine White's centre too soon by 8...P-B3, White can build up an extremely active position by sacrificing a pawn: (8...P-B3?) 9 P-K6! N-N5 10 R-B1 B×P 11 P-QR3 N-R3 12 N-B3 P-B3 13 N-K4 B-B4 14 B-Q3 with a clear advantage. The same can be said of 8...Q-Q2 (preparing for . . .O-O-O): 9 N-B3 B-N5 10 P-Q5 B×N 11 Q×B N×KP 12 Q-K4! N-N5 13 O-O-O again with a clear advantage, Wolf and Kaufmann-Honlinger and Glass, consulation game 1934.

A different yet equally unsuccessful way for Black to try for an early counter-attack is 8...N-N5. After 9 R-B1 P-B4 10 P-Q5 P-K3 11 P-QR3 P×P 12 Q-B3, 12...N-B7+? loses to 13 R×N B×R 14 P×P N-B5 15 B×N Q-R5+ 16 P-KN3 Q×B 17 KN-K2 B-N3 18 O-O O-O-O 19 P-Q6 with an overwhelming position. If instead Black tries 12...N-Q6+ 13 B×N B×B he still fares none too well after 14 P×P P-B5 15 P-Q6 Q-Q2 16 N-R3.

9 N-B3(*60*)

Black now has five plausible moves at his disposal.
We shall examine in turn:

A 9...B-KN5
B 9...B-QN5
C 9...Q-Q2
D 9...N-N5
E 9...B-K2

A

1 P-K4 N-KB3 2 P-K5 N-Q4 3 P-QB4 N-N3 4 P-Q4 P-Q3 5 P-B4 P×P 6 BP×P N-B3 7 B-K3 B-B4 8 N-QB3 P-K3 9 N-B3

9 ...	B-KN5

A rarely played move.

10 Q-Q2!	

Breaking the pin at once and thereby rendering Black's second move with his QB somewhat ineffectual.

10   ...   B-K2

Konstantinopolsky's suggestion 10...N-R4 11 P-QN3 B-N5 is best met by 12 B-K2 and 13 O-O when the black knight on R4 is left out of play and the pressure exerted by the bishop at QN5 has been minimized.

The only consistent attempt by Black (10...B×N) to justify his previous move, concedes the advantage of the two bishops without extracting any compensation. The game Henneberger-Trueb, 1941 continued: 10...B×N 11 P×B Q-R5+ 12 B-B2 Q-K2 13 O-O-O O-O-O 14 P-B4 Q-N5 15 P-QR3 Q-N6 16 Q-B2! Q×Q+ 17 K×Q B-K2 18 P-N4 and White's game was positionally overwhelming because of his substantial advantage in space and the mobility of his bishops. After 18...P-N4 19 P-Q5 KP×P 20 QBP×P N-N1 21 P-B5! the white army soon crashed through.

11   B-K2   O-O
12   O-O   P-B3
13   P×P   B×P

Were it Black's move and were his QB on KB4 instead of KN5, the position would be a standard one for the Four Pawns Attack. In that position Black's choice normally lies amongst the moves 13...Q-Q2, 13...Q-K1 and 13...R-B2, with the plan of building up pressure on White's QP. The text position is therefore one that can be thought of as arising out of a normal Four Pawns Attack though with the exception that Black has played the unthematic 13...B-KN5 in place of one of the three more usual moves. The result is that Black's counterplay, inevitably directed along the Q-file, has not yet got going, and White can simply build up his position by 14 QR-Q1 (±)

B

9 ...   B-QN5(*61*)

1 P-K4 N-KB3 2 P-K5 N-Q4 3 P-QB4 N-N3 4 P-Q4 P-Q3 5 P-B4 P×P 6 BP×P N-B3 7 B-K3 B-B4 8 N-QB3 P-K3 9 N-B3

61

10	B-K2	O-O

Tartakower pointed out that 10...B-N5 11 O-O B.KN5×N 12 R×B Q-Q2 13 P-QR3 is clearly better for White, the reasons being his two bishops, his strong central pawn mass and the lead in development which will pave the way for an attack against the black king once the second player has castled. Other possibilities are 10...N-R4 11 P-B5 N3-B5 12 B-QB1 O-O 13 O-O± and 10...Q-Q2 11 O-O N-R4 12 N-Q2 O-O-O 13 P-B5±.

11	O-O	B×N
12	P×B	N-R4
13	P-B5	N3-B5
14	B-N5	Q-Q2

Not 14...P-KB3 15 P×P P×P 16 B-R6 R-B2 17 B×N N×B 18 N-R4 B-N3 19 N×B P×N 20 Q-Q3!

15	N-R4	P-KR3
16	B-B1	B-R2
17	R-B3	Q-K2
18	R-R3	

With a dangerous attack. Prada-Esnaola, corres 1959.

C

1 P-K4 N-KB3 2 P-K5 N-Q4 3 P-QB4 N-N3 4 P-Q4 P-Q3 5 P-B4 P×P 6 BP×P N-B3 7 B-K3 B-B4 8 N-QB3 P-K3 9 N-B3

9 ...	Q-Q2 (62)

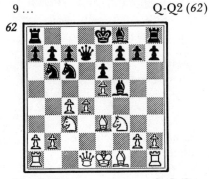

10	B-K2	O-O-O

The only consistent continuation. Alternatives are:

a) 10...B-QN5 11 O-O B×N 12 P×B N-R4 13 N-Q2 O-O 14 R-B3 P-KB3 (on 14...B-N5 15 R-N3 B×B 16 Q×B White also has good attacking prospects on the K-side) 15 P×P R×P 16 R-N3 R-N3 17 Q-K1 Q-R5 18 R×R B×R 19 B-B4 N4×P 20 B-N4 R-K1 21 B×BP N-Q4 22 B×P+ K-R1 23 Q-B2! with a safe extra pawn, Tribushevsky-Bastrikov, USSR 1959;

b) 10...N-R4 11 P-QN3 B-QN5 12 Q-Q2 R-QB1 (not 12...P-B4 13 P×P
Q×Q+ 14 B×Q B×P 15 N-QN5 and Black loses at least an exchange) 13
O-O P-B4 14 QR-Q1 P×P 15 N×P B-K5 16 Q-B1 and again the loose
knight on . . .QR4 proves a handicap (16...B×N 17 Q×B with a double
threat), Ullmann-Trinks, Germany 1923;

c) 10...B-KN5 11 O-O R-Q1 (or 10...R-Q1 11 O-O B-KN5) 12 N-KN5!
N×BP (12...B×B can be met by 13 Q×B! because 13...N×QP 14 B×N
Q×B+ 15 K-R1 leaves Black helpless against the threat to his KB2) 13
B-B2 B×B 14 Q×B B-K2 (not 14...N-N3 15 QR-Q1±) 15 Q-R5! P-KN3
16 Q-R6 N×QP 17 Q-N7 R-KB1 18 N×RP with a won game for White,
Estrin-Oakley, corres 1962.

11   O-O   P-B3

11...B-K2? is so slow that White's central push is virtually decisive: 12
P-Q5! P×P 13 B×N RP×B 14 P×P N-N5 (or 14...B-B4+ 15 K-R1 N-K2
16 N-KR4±) 15 N-Q4 P-KN3 (15...B-B4 loses to 16 R×B! Q×R 17 B-
N4) 16 N×B P×N 17 R×P! N×QP 18 P-K6! P×P 19 R×N, and if 19...P×R
then 20 B-N4 wins the black queen.

11...B-KN5 is an attempt to put further pressure on White's QP, but
again White has a forceful rejoinder: 12 P-B5! N-Q4 (12...N-R1 13 Q-
R4 and 12...B×N?? 13 P×N B×B 14 P×RP are both quick routes by
which Black can commit suicide) 13 N×N Q×N 14 N-N5! B×B 15 Q×B
N×QP 16 B×N Q×B+ 17 K-R1 Q-Q7 18 Q×Q R×Q 19 R×P B×P 20
N×KP B-N3 21 N×NP B-Q5 22 P-K6 B×NP 23 R-K1 B×N 24 R×B with
a probably winning ending. Analysis by Doroshkevisch.

12   P-Q5!

This thrust, originally suggested by Mikenas, causes a grave
disruption within Black's ranks and opens the way for a direct assault
against the black king.

12   ...   N×KP

Again the alternatives merely result in White gaining an
overwhelming position:

a) 12...Q-B2? 13 Q-N3 KP×P (or 13...N-K2 14 P-Q6 QBP×P 15 B×N
P×B 16 P×QP R×P 17 N-QN5+) 14 B×N RP×B 15 BP×P N-N5 (if
15...N-K2 16 P-K6) 16 P-K6± J. Schmidt-Lingier, corres 1956;

b) 12...Q-K1 13 B×N RP×B 14 Q-R4 with a strong attack;

c) 12...KP×P? 13 B×N BP×B (if 13...RP×B, 14 Q-R4 followed by 15 N-
QN5 is very strong)14 BP×P N-K2 (or 14...N×P 15 N×N P×N 16 R×B!)
15 P×P P×P 16 N-KR4 B-N3 17 R×P and White threatens the
ubiquitous 18 B-N4.

13   N×N   P×N

             14   P-QR4!

The most direct method of attack.

             14   ...   K-N1

Black must make way for his knight to retreat, since 14...P-QR4? fails to Shashin's suggestion 15 N-N5 B-QN5 16 P-Q6! P-B4 17 Q-B1 to be followed by B-Q2 when White still has a strong attack.

14...P×P? meets with an even more drastic refutation in 15 R×B! Q×R 16 B-N4 (what else!).

             15   P-R5   N-B1
             16   Q-N3   P-B3
             17   P-R6

White has a clear advantage. The game Teschner-Maier, Berlin 1962, continued: 17...P-QN3 (17...KP×P 18 R×B!) 18 QR-Q1 BP×P 19 P×P B-Q3 20 P-N4 B-N3 (if 20...P×P 21 R×B P-Q5 22 B-QN5!) 21 P×P Q-K2 22 Q-Q5 P-K5 23 Q-B6 Q-QB2 24 Q×Q+ B×Q 25 R-Q7 and White had a winning endgame.

D

1 P-K4 N-KB3 2 P-K5 N-Q4 3 P-QB4 N-N3 4 P-Q4 P-Q3 5 P-B4 P×P 6 BP×P N-B3 7 B-K3 B-B4 8 N-QB3 P-K3 9 N-B3

             9 ...   N-N5 (*63*)

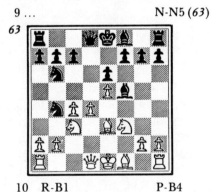

63

             10   R-B1   P-B4

Black's last two moves introduce a system pioneered by Alekhine, the aim of which is to shatter White's pawn centre and start the tactics before the first player has had time to castle. It is true that if White does not play carefully he can meet with a variety of horrors, but with accurate and incisive play he can be sure of a significant and lasting advantage.

             11   B-K2

Now Black can choose between:
D1 11...B-N5

D2 11...P×P?
D3 11...B-K2
D4 11...Q-Q2?

D1

1 P-K4 N-KB3 2 P-K5 N-Q4 3 P-QB4 N-N3 4 P-Q4 P-Q3 5 P-B4 P×P 6 BP×P N-B3 7 B-K3 B-B4 8 N-QB3 P-K3 9 N-B3 N-N5 10 R-B1 P-B4 11 B-K2

11	...	B-N5
12	B-N5!	P-B3

Alternatives are:

a) 12...B-K2 13 B×B Q×B 14 N-K4 O-O 15 P×P N-Q2 16 P-QR3 N-QB3 17 Q-Q6± (Schwarz); or

b) 12...Q-Q2 13 P-Q5 B×N 14 P×B P×P 15 P×P P-B5 16 P-B4 N5×QP 17 N×N N×N 18 B×P B-N5+ 19 K-B2 B-B4+ 20 K-N3 (Bagirov) when White's powerful bishops give him the upper hand.

13	KP×P	NP×P
14	N-K5	P×B
15	B×B	Q×P
16	B-R5+	K-K2
17	Q×Q	P×Q
18	O-O!	P×N
19	R.QB1-Q1	N5-Q4
20	P×N	KP×P

Or 20...N×P 21 P×P with the threat of 22 P-B4

21	N-B7	R-KN1
22	B-N4	K-K1
23	R.Q1-K1+	B-K2
24	N-Q6+	K-Q1
25	N×P+	K-K1
26	B-R5+	K-Q2
27	R-B7	N-B1
28	P×P	

With a won game for White. Analysis by Boleslavsky.

D2

1 P-K4 N-KB3 2 P-K5 N-Q4 3 P-QB4 N-N3 4 P-Q4 P-Q3 5 P-B4 P×P 6 BP×P N-B3 7 B-K3 B-B4 8 N-QB3 P-K3 9 N-B3 N-N5 10 R-B1 P-B4 11 B-K2

11	...	P×P? (64)

64

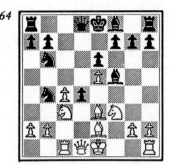

| 12 | N×P | B-N3 |

After 12...N-B3 13 N×B Q×Q+ 14 R×Q P×N, the ending is much better for White. e.g. 15 O-O B-K2 16 R×P P-N3 17 R-B4 N×KP 18 R-K4 P-B3 19 P-B5!±. Bronstein-Mikenas, USSR Championship 1949, concluded: 19...N3-Q2 20 N-Q5! K-B1 (if 20...B-Q1 21 B-QN5 O-O 22 B×N N×B 23 N-K7+ B×N 24 R×N B-Q1 25 B-R6±±) 21 N-B7! R-Q1 22 N-K6+ K-B2 23 N×R+ R×N 24 R4-Q4 K-K3 25 P-QN4 B-B1 26 B-QN5 P-B4 27 B-KB4 1-O.

12...Q-B2 13 P-B5! is another line that gives White an almost winning advantage:

a) 13...Q×BP 14 N×B Q×P 15 B×N winning a piece

b) 13...B×P 14 N×B P×N 15 B×B Q×B 16 N-N5 followed by 17 N-B7+ winning;

c) 13...Q×KP 14 N×B P×N 15 B-Q4 again winning a piece, or

d) 13...N-Q2 (relatively best) 14 P-QR3 N-QB3 (if 14...Q×KP then 15 N×B followed by B-Q4 etc.) 15 N×B P×N 16 N-Q5 Q-Q1 (if 16...Q×KP 17 B-KB4 wins at once) 17 O-O P-KN3 18 Q-Q2 with a great advantage for White, Barden-Fazekas, Nottingham, 1954.

| | 13 | P-B5! |

This strong move suggested by Levenfish takes advantage of Black's lack of co-ordination.

| 13 | ... | N-Q2 |

13...B×P loses to 14 B-QN5+ and now if 14...K-B1 then 15 N×P+ P×N 16 B×B+ or if 14...N-B3 then 15 N×N Q×Q+ 16 N×Q! winning a piece.

On 13...N3-Q4, 14 Q-R4+ is killing.

14	Q-R4	N-Q6+
15	B×N	B×B
16	R-Q1	B-N3
17	P-B6	

with a colossal advantage.

D3

1 P-K4 N-KB3 2 P-K5 N-Q4 3 P-QB4 N-N3 4 P-Q4 P-Q3 5 P-B4 P×P 6 BP×P N-B3 7 B-K4 B-B4 8 N-QB3 P-K3 9 n-B3 N-N5 10 R-B1 P-B4 11 B-K2

11	...	B-K2 *(65)*

This is undoubtedly the best of Black's four options.

65

12	P-QR3	P×P
13	N×P	N-B3

Now the position is almost identical to that arising in the previous variation, note to Black's twelfth move. The difference here is that White has played P-QR3 and Black . . .B-K2. It is this difference, Black's development being one move further advanced, that reduces White's advantage, but the advantage remaining is still significant.

14	N×B	P×N

On 14...Q×Q+ 15 R×Q P×N it is logical for White to take advantage of his 'wasted' move (P-QR3) and the following continuation is indicated: 16 B×N P×B 17 N-Q5 (now 17...B-N5+ is not possible whereas with White's QRP on R2 instead of R3 Black would be able to play 17...B-N5+ 18 N×B N×N 19 P-QR3 N-B3 when Black has at least a level game) 17...R-Q1 18 N-B7+ K-B1 19 O-O±.

15	O-O	O-O

Or 15...N×KP 16 R×P Q×Q+ 17 N×Q! N3-Q2 18 N-B3 P-KN3 19 R5-B1± (threatening 20 N-Q5) Tartakower-Colle, 1926.

16	R×P	P-N3
17	R-B1	B-N4!
18	B-B5!	R-K1!

18...B×R? leaves Black extremely weak on the dark squares surrounding his king: 19 Q×B! R-K1 20 N-K4 R×P 21 N-B6+ K-N2 22 N-N4! and White has a clear plus, e.g. 22...Q-N4 23 N×R Q×N 24 B-K3±

| 19 | Q×Q | QR×Q |
| 20 | R.QB1-Q1 | N×KP |

The ending after 20...R-Q7 21 R×R B×R 22 B-Q6! B×N 23 P×B N×KP 24 P-B5 N-Q4 25 R-B1 R-K3 26 B-B1 is also much better for White. Petrov-Fine, Kemeri 1937, concluded: 26...P-QR3? (better would be 26...N-K6) 27 R-N1 P-QN4 28 P×Pep R×B 29 P-N7 N-QB3 30 P-B4! N-K6 31 R-N6! R-Q8 32 K-B2 R×B+ 33 K×N N-N1 34 R-Q6? (A quicker way to win was 34 K-Q2! the text was an error made in time trouble) 34...R-K8+ 35 K-Q4? (35 K-Q2! is still superior) 35...K-B1? 36 R-Q8+ R-K1 37 R-B8! K-K2 38 K-Q5 R-Q1+ 39 R×R K×R 40 K-Q6! 1-0.

21	N-K4!	R×R
22	B×R!	B-K2
23	P-QN3	B×B+
24	N×B	R-K2
25	B-B2	

The ending is somewhat better for White. Keres-Sajtar, Prague 1943.

D4

1 P-K4 N-KB3 2 P-K5 N-Q4 3 P-QB4 N-N3 4 P-Q4 P-Q3 5 P-B4 P×P 6 BP×P N-B3 7 B-K3 B-B4 8 N-QB3 P-K3 9 N-B3 N-N5 10 R-B1 P-B4 11 B-K2

| 11 | ... | Q-Q2? (*66*) |

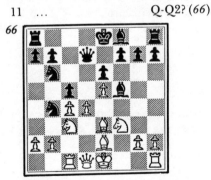

66

This move is completely wasted.

12	P-QR3	P×P
13	N×P	N-B3
14	N×B	P×N

After 14...Q×Q+ 15 R×Q White is a tempo ahead of the Bronstein-Milenas game mentioned in variation D2.

| 15 | Q-B2 | N×KP |
| 16 | R-Q1 | Q-B3 |

Not 16...Q-K3? 17 N-Q5!

17	P-B5	N3-Q2
18	B-QN5±	

Medina-Ganzo, 1942.

E

1 P-K4 N-KB3 2 P-K5 N-Q4 3 P-QB4 N-N3 4 P-Q4 P-Q3 5 P-B4 P×P 6 BP×P N-B3 7 B-K3 B-B4 8 N-QB3 P-K3 9 N-B3

9 ...   B-K2 (*67*)

67

10   P-Q5!!

This is the move that was brought into the limelight by Velimirovic in his game with Gipslis at Havana 1971. It leads to sharp play in all variations and poses difficult problems to 9...B-K2 which for so many years has been the main line of the Four Pawns Attack.

We now consider:
E1 10...P×P
E2 10...N-N5

E1

1 P-K4 n-KB3 2 P-K5 N-Q4 3 P-QB4 N-N3 4 P-Q4 P-Q3 5 P-B4 P×P 6 BP×P N-B3 7 B-K3 B-B4 8 N-QB3 P-K3 9 N-B3 B-K2 10 P-Q5!!

10	...	P×P
11	P×P	N-N5
12	N-Q4	

Forcing Black to make a decision about the future of his QB while at the same time guarding the square QB2 and preparing for the possibility of a later P-K6.

12   ...   B-Q2

The alternatives are certainly no better:
a) 12...B-N3 13 B-QN5+ K-B1 14 O-O (threatening 15 N-K6+ winning the queen) 14...K-N1 15 N-B5 B×N, Stanciu-Partos, Romania 1971,

concluded 16 R×B!(±) N5×QP (or 16...N3×P 17 Q-N3 P-QB3 18 P-QR3 N-R3 19 N×N P×N 20 B×N P×B 21 R1-KB1±) 17 B×N! N×B 18 Q-N3 B-B4+ 19 K-R1 Q-K2 20 N-R4!! Q-K3 (If 20...N×N 21 B-B4 R-KB1 22 QR-KB1 wins) 21 N×B Q×R 22 R-KB1 Q-R4 23 B-K2! Q-N3 24 B-Q3 Q-R4 25 P-N4! 1-O.

b) 12...B-QB1 13 B-QN5+ P-QB3 14 P×P O-O 15 O-O P-QR3 16 P×P B×P 17 B-K2 N5-Q4 18 B-B2! B-N4 (If 18...N×N 19 P×N N-Q4 20 Q-N3 R-N1 21 B-B3±) 19 N-B5! B-QB3 20 N-K4 N-KB5 21 B-B3 N3-Q4 22 N-Q4!± Ghizdavu-Suta, Romania 1970. The game concluded 22...B-Q2? (22...B-N2 was better but then 23 N-Q6 leaves Black in bad shape) 23 N×B Q×N 24 B×N QR-Q1 25 Q-B3! B-N5 26 B-R4! Q×B 27 Q×N R×B 28 N-B5! 1-O.

c) 12...Q-Q2? 13 P-QR3! N.N5×P 14 N×B and White wins a piece.

13	P-K6	P×P
14	P×P	B-QB3
15	Q-N4	B-KR5+
16	P-KN3!	B×R

16...N(either)-Q4 loses to 17 B-KR6!! P×B 18 Q-R5+ etc.

| 17 | O-O-O | Q-B3 |

In Williams-Cafferty, British Championship 1971, Black played 17...B-KB3? and lost by force: 18 N-B5 N5-Q4 19 N×P+ B×N 20 Q-R5+ K-K2 21 B-B5+ K×P 22 B-KR3+ 1-O.

| 18 | P×B | O-O |
| 19 | B-K2 | P-B4! |

The only satisfactory move.

20	B-KN5	Q-K4
21	P-K7	P×N
22	P×RQ+	R×Q
23	Q×P	Q×Q
24	R×Q	N-B3
25	R-KB4	

White has slightly the better endgame prospects because of the advantage of the two bishops. It would be a mistake for Black to exchange rooks at the moment.

E2

1 P-K4 N-KB3 2 P-K5 N-Q4 3 P-QB4 N-N3 4 P-Q4 P-Q3 5 P-B4 P×P 6 BP×P N-B3 7 B-K3 B-B4 8 N-QB3 P-K3 9 N-B3 B-K2 10 P-Q5!!

| 10 | ... | N-N5 (*68*) |

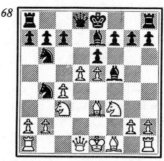

68

This was the continuation in the Velimirovic-Gipslis game.

           11   R-B1!   P-KB3

After 11...P×P 12 P-QR3 N×P 13 B×N P×B 14 P×N, Black has
insufficient compensation for the lost piece.

11...O-O may seem natural but it can be refuted by 12 P-QR3 N-R3
13 B-Q3! when Black's position is already beyond repair. Parma-
Mihaljcisin, Sarajevo 1970, concluded 13...B-B4 (if 13...B×B 14 Q×B
N-B4 15 B×N B×B 16 P-QN4 and Black has no room to move) 14
B.K3×B N×B 15 B×B P×B 16 P-QN4 N-K5 17 Q-Q4 P-QB3 18 P×P P×P
19 N×N P×N (or 19...Q×Q 20 N×Q P×N 21 N×P KR-K1 22 P-B5 N-Q2
23 K-K2 with a won ending.) 20 Q×P R-B1 21 N-Q4 R-K1 22 O-O Q-B2
23 KR-K1 N-Q2 24 P-K6 N-B3 25 Q-B5 R.B1-Q1 26 P×P+ Q×P 27
N×P R-Q7 28 N-K5 Q-N2 29 N-B3 R1-K7 30 R×R R×R 31 Q-Q3 Q-K2
32 R-Q1 1-O.

           12   P-QR3   N-R3
           13   P-KN4!

An incredible move, but one that is typical of Velimirovic's
ingenuity. White sacrifices a pawn in order to open up the KN-file for
an attack against the black king.

           13   ...   B×NP

If 13...B-N3, 14 QP×P wins a pawn for nothing.

           14   R-KN1   P-KB4?

Better is 14...B-R4, when 15 B-K2 (threatening 16 N-Q4) leaves
White with ample compensation for the pawn.

           15   P-R3   B×N

A few rounds later, in the same tournament, one of the local players,
Rodriguez, 'improved' with 15...B-R5+ 16 K-Q2 B-R4. His opponent,
grandmaster Tringov, was not in the least put out by the new course of
events and the game ended very rapidly: 17 R×P P×P 18 P×P N×P 19
Q-R4+ P-B3 20 Q×B B×N 21 B-KN5 Q-R4 22 P-N4 1-O.

	16	Q×B	O-O
	17	R-B2	

White's attack is devastating.

	17	...	Q-Q2
	18	R-Q2!	QR-K1
	19	P-Q6±±	

The Velimirovic-Gipslis game concluded 19...P×P 20 Q-R5! R-B1 21 P-B5! (threatening 22 B-QN5) 21...R×P 22 B×R? (a time trouble error. Better is 22 R2-N2 R-KB2 23 B×R N×B 24 B-N5! Q-B2 25 Q×R+ K×Q 26 R×P+ K-B1 27 R-N8+ K-B2 28 R1-N7 mate) 22...N×B 23 R2-N2 P-N4! 24 B-N5 Q-Q1 25 P-N4? (25 P×P B-B3 26 N-K2 threatening N-B4 would still win. Now the game should have been drawn) 25...N4-Q2 26 P×P B-B3 27 N-K2 N-K4! 28 N-B4 Q×P?? (28...K-R1! 29 N×P Q-B1! draws by perpetual check after 30 P-Q7 Q-B8+) 29 R×P+ K-R1 30 Q×P+ 1-0.

10 Pirc/Modern Defence

The Pirc Defence (1 P-K4 P-Q3 2 P-Q4 N-KB3 3 N-QB3 P-KN3) is an ambitious set-up for Black which tempts forwards White's centre pawns in the hope of undermining them. There is relatively little information to digest on this defence in its main lines since this whole strategy for Black only became 'respectable' as the result of victories by Soviet grandmasters with it in the 1962 Candidates' Tournament at Curacao. Thus we can see that anyone adopting the Pirc Defence (or the alternative move order 1 P-K4 P-KN3 2 P-Q4 B-N2 3 N-QB3 P-Q3) will be involved in a highly up-to-date opening system, the theory of which is still expanding.

For White we recommend against the Pirc the Robert Byrne method (with B-KN5) which combines the virtues of solidity and aggression and which creates a tense position with mutual chances. The alternative methods for White (dealt with under Black section) tend to err on the side of attempting too much, or too little.

Austrian Attack

1 P-K4 P-Q3 2 P-Q4 N-KB3 3 N-QB3 P-KN3

4	P-B4	B-N2
5	N-B3	P-B4 (*69*)

69

White has set up a broad pawn centre which Black immediately attacks. 5...P-B4 enforces an asymmetric pawn structure at a very early stage and so ensures a strategically unbalanced struggle. White has four main possibilities here:

A 6 B-N5+
B 6 P-K5
C 6 P-Q5
D 6 P×P

A

1 P-K4 P-Q3 2 P-Q4 N-KB3 3 N-QB3 P-KN3 4 P-B4 B-N2 5 N-B3 P-B4

6	B-N5+	B-Q2
7	P-K5	N-N5
8	P-K6	

Or:

a) 8 B×B+? (White's centre disintegrates after this) 8...Q×B 9 N-KN5 BP×P 10 P-K6 P×P 11 Q×N P×N 12 N×KP P×P 13 N×B+ K-B2 14 Q×Q P×B=Q+ 15 R×Q N×Q 16 R-QN1 N-B4 0-1 Purdy-R.Byrne, USA 1968.

b) 8 N-N5 B×B 9 Q×N B-Q2 10 P-K6 B×KP 11 N×B P×N 12 P×P B×N+! 13 P×B Q-R4± Lee-Suttles, Havana 1966. Once again collapse of his centre.

c) 8 P-KR3 when Black can offer a promising exchange sacrifice with 8...BP×P 9 Q×P P×P 10 Q-Q5! P-K5! 11 N-N5 N-KR3 12 Q×NP 0-0 13 Q×R (so far Kurajica-Keene, Wijk aan Zee 1974) 13...B×N+! 14 P×B B×B 15 Q×RP Q-B1 or 15 Q×KP N-B4 and White will have great difficulty in co-ordinating his pieces.

8	...	B×B
9	KP×P+	

9 N-N5 P-B4! is hopeless for White.

9	...	K-Q2

This king journey looks odd but the line is very playable for Black.

10	N×B

The piece sacrifice 10 N-N5?! is unsound. Jensen-Keene, The Hague 1967, continued 10...P-KR4 11 N×B Q-R4+ 12 N-QB3 P×P 13 Q-K2 P×N 14 Q-K6+ K-Q1 15 P-N4 Q-N3 16 R-B1 when Black could have gone in for immediate counter-attack with 16...N-QB3 e.g. 17 Q×NP N×NP 18 Q×B N×BP+ 19 K-Q1 N7-K6+ 20 B×N Q×B 21 Q×R+ K-Q2 and wins.

10	...	Q-R4+
11	N-B3	P×P
12	N×P	B×N *(70)*

Thus far White's moves have been forced, but now he has a choice of recaptures:

a) 13 Q×N+ Q-KB4 is in Black's favour e.g. 14 Q-B3 N-B3 15 N-K2 Q-K3 16 P-B3 B-N3 17 B-Q2 QR-KB1 18 P-QN3 R×P 19 O-O-O P-KR4 20 P-KR3 P-R5 21 KR-K1 Q-B3 22 B-K3 B×B+ 23 Q×B R-R4!± (White's knight is tied to the protection of his KBP and his castled position has been slightly weakened. These factors outweigh his slight pressure on the central files.) Tringov-Benko, Sarajevo 1967 or 14 Q×Q+ P×Q 15 N-K2 N-B3 16 P-B3 B-N3 17 P-QN3 QR-KB1 18 B-N2 R×P 19 O-O-O P-KR4∓ Harding-Botterill, Oxford University Championship 1968.

b)   13   Q×B   N-QB3
                     14   Q-Q1

Alternatives are weaker e.g.

b1) 14 Q-Q5 Q×Q (now Black's centralized king is well-placed for the endgame) 15 N×Q N-Q5 16 K-Q2 KR-KB1 17 P-KR3 N-R3 18 P-QN3 R×P 19 B-N2 N-K3 20 KR-KB1 QR-KB1∓ Zuidema-Suttles, Havana 1966, or

b2) 14 Q-Q2 KR-KB1 15 P-KR3 N-B3 16 P-QN3 R×P 17 P-KN4 P-R4 18 P-N5 N-K1 19 B-N2 N-N2 20 O-O-O N-K3 and White's KBP is too weak, Zuckerman-Benkö, New York 1967.

                     14   ...   Q-R4

White hardly has anything better than 15 Q-B3 KR-KB1 16 B-Q2 N-B3! when the endgame should be slightly in Black's favour in view of the weak pawn at KB4 and the lack of scope for White's QB.

B

1 P-K4 P-Q3 2 P-Q4 N-KB3 3 N-QB3 P-KN4 4 P-B4 B-N2 5 N-B3 P-B4

                     6 P-K5 *(71)*

71

The displacement of Black's KN by means of this thrust forms a recurring theme of White's play against the Pirc/Modern Defence.

6 ...	N3-Q2
7 KP×P	

Other moves pose Black fewer problems

a) 7 B-B4 BP×P 8 Q×P O-O 9 P-KR4 P×P and White does not have much compensation for the pawn, Beghan-Shaskin, Sverdlovsk 1969.

b) 7 P-K6!? A pawn sacrifice designed to cramp Black's game but it voluntarily liquidates White's own centre. Play could continue: 7...P×KP 8 N-KN5 N-KB3 9 P×P N-B3 10 B-Q3 P×P 11 O-O O-O 12 Q-K1 N-QN5 13 N×KP N×B 14 P×N B×N 15 Q×B+ K-R1 16 B-K3 R-B1∓ Hartston-Timman, Hastings 1973-4. Black is threatening ...R-B3, driving White's queen to the awkward square KR3 (otherwise ...N-KN5). This, together with pressure on the Q-file and long diagonal, more than balances the isolated KP.

c) 7 QP×P P×KP when 8 P×P N×KP 9 Q×Q+ K×Q is in Black's favour due to his better pawns, and 8 B-B4 O-O 9 O-O as in Timofeeva-Faprindashivili, Vilnius 1958, when 9...N-QB3 is ∓ (Black's centre pawns backed up by the strong KB are more mobile than White's Q-side majority).

7 ...	O-O!

Black sacrifices a pawn for dangerous chances. 8 P×KP P×BP Q-R4!? and Black has promising chances in the complications; or 8 B-K3 Q-N3 9 P×KP R-K1 and Black will regain material with a dangerous initiative since White's king is exposed in the centre, Matulovic-Adorjan, Wijk aan Zee 1974.) 8... Q×P+ 9 B-K2 (9 Q-K2 Q×Q+! 10 N×Q N-QB3 11 P-B3 R-K1 12 P-Q5 N-K2 13 P-B4 N-N3 when Black will recover his pawn and still have the better development.) 9...P×P 10 N×P R-K1 suits Black well for White is now unable to castle (11 O-O? Q-B4) and he has a good lead in development. This represents typical Pirc/Modern play for Black in that he is prepared to invest material to ensure himself of the initiative and to enhance the scope of his powerful fianchettoed bishop.

C

1 P-K4 P-Q3 2 P-Q4 N-KB3 3 N-QB3 P-KN3 4 P-B4 B-N2 5 N-B3 P-B4

6 P-Q5	O-O
7 B-Q3	

If 7 B-K2 then still 7...P-K3.

7 ...	P-K3
8 P×P	P×P
9 O-O	N-B3=

Black has a promising position in the centre.

D

1 P-K4 P-Q3 2 P-Q4 N-KB3 3 N-QB3 P-KN3 4 P-B4 B-N2 5 N-B3 P-B4

6 P×P	Q-R4! (72)

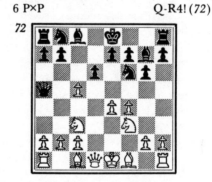

Now 7 P×P? fails to 7...N×P! unleashing the force of the fianchettod KB, so:
D1 7 B-N5+
D2 7 N-Q2
D3 7 Q-Q3
D4 7 B-Q3
D1
1 P-K4 P-Q3 2 P-Q4 N-KB3 3 N-QB3 P-KN3 4 P-B4 B-N2 5 N-B3 P-B4 6 P×P Q-R4!

7 B-N5+	B-Q2
8 B×B+	

8 Q-K2? N×P! 9 B×B+ N×B 10 Q×N B×N+ 11 P×B Q×P.B6+ 12 K-B2 Q×R 13 P×P O-O 14 P×P KR-K1 15 Q×QNP N-B3 16 R-Q1 K-N2 and

White is lost, Kliavins-Kampenus, Riga 1956.

8 ...	QN×B
9 O-O	Q×BP+
10 K-R1	O-O

Honfi-Hort, Monaco 1969, continued 11 Q-K2 QR-B1 12 B-K3 Q-B5 13 Q-Q3 P-QR3 14 QR-K1 KR-Q1 15 P-K5 N-K1 16 Q×Q R×Q 17 R-Q1 P-K3 18 R-B2 R1-B1 19 P-QR3 P-QN4 20 B-B1 P-Q4 when Black's pressure on the QB-file gives him the advantage.

D2

1 P-K4 P-Q3 2 P-Q4 N-KB3 3 N-QB3 P-KN3 4 P-B4 B-N2 5 N-B3 P-B4 6 P×P Q-R4!

7 N-Q2

Now O'Kelly-Farre, Torremolinos 1961, went 7...Q×BP 8 N-N3 Q-B2 9 B-K2 QN-Q2 10 B-K3 N-N3 11 B-Q4 O-O 12 O-O B-Q2 13 K-R1 B-B3 14 B-Q3 P-K4 15 P×P P×P 16 B-B5 KR-K1 with an equal game — White can make little headway on the KB-file.

D3

1 P-K4 P-Q3 2 P-Q4 N-KB3 3 N-QB3 P-KN3 4 P-B4 B-N2 5 N-B3 P-B4 6 P×P Q-R4!

7 Q-Q3 (*73*)

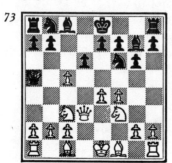

73

7 ...	Q×BP
8 B-K3	Q-QR4
9 N-Q2	

Or 9 B-K2 O-O 10 O-O P-QR3 11 K-R1 QN-Q2 12 P-QR3 N-B4 13 Q-Q2 Q-B2 14 B-Q3 P-K3 15 Q-K1 N-N5∓ Geller-Nikolaevsky, Kiev 1958. Black's pressure on the Q-side is worth more than White's rather vague chances on the other wing.

Black should now play 9...O-O and follow up with ...QN-Q2...P-QR3 and ...N-B4 with a perfectly satisfactory game.

D4

1 P-K4 P-Q3 2 P-Q4 N-KB3 3 N-QB3 P-KN3 4 P-B4 B-N2 5 N-B3 P-B4 6 P×P Q-R4!

7 B-Q3 *(74)*

The usual move.

74

7 ...   Q×BP
8 Q-K2   B-N5

By pinning and then exchanging off White's KN, Black increases his influence over the vital squares ...K4 and ...Q5. The game could continue 9 B-K3 Q-QR4 10 O-O N-B3 11 P-KR3 B×N 12 Q×B O-O 13 P-R3 N-Q2 (unmasking the bishop) 14 B-Q2 Q-N3+ 15 K-R1 N-B4 16 QR-N1 N×B 17 P×N Adorjan-Suttles, Hastings 1973/4. Here Black can maintain a good position with 17...P-B4! preventing K-side aggression with P-KB5.

White Plays B-QB4—the Holmov System

1 P-K4 P-Q3 2 P-Q4 N-KB3 3 N-QB3 P-KN3
4 B-QB4

The obvious purpose of this move is to secure as dynamic a rôle as possible for the KB. The bishop exerts threats on the diagonal QR2-KN8 but on the minus side it is also vulnerable to attack by means of ...P-QB3 and ...P-Q4, or ...P-QN4, or ...even sometimes the little fork-trick combination ...N×KP followed by ...P-Q4, hitting two pieces. These possibilities reveal the advantages connected with Black's decision to delay committing his central pawns to any rigid configuration.

4 ...   B-N2 *(75)*

75

Now White may choose between the moves:
A 5 Q-K2
B 5 P-B4
C N-B3

A

1 P-K4 P-Q3 2 P-Q4 N-KB3 3 N-QB3 P-KN3 4 B-QB4 B-N2

     5 Q-K2

White intends to launch an immediate attack by means of the push P-K5.

     5 ...   N-B3!

A strong move taking advantage of the unprotected QP. White faces a difficult problem here. After 6 P-K5 N×QP 7 P×N N×Q 8 P×B R-KN1 9 KN×N R×P Black is better with his queen and two pawns taking on three minor pieces. The more cautious 6 B-K3 allows Black to obtain a fine position with 6...N×KP 7 B×P+ (7 N×N P-Q4 and Black regains the piece with a free game) 7...K×B 8 N×N R-K1 followed by ...K-N1. Black's position is flexible with the bishop pair, and artificial castling is as good as the genuine article in this case. 6 N-B3 B-N5 does not solve the problem of the QP's defence for White, while 6 P-Q5? blocks the KB's diagonal and is answered by 6...N-QN1 with a sound position. Black's KB would represent an appreciating investment on the KR1--QR8 diagonal which is rapidly being emptied of White's pawns.

B

1 P-K4 P-Q3 2 P-Q4 N-KB3 3 N-QB3 P-KN3 4 B-QB4 B-N2

     5 P-B4   N×P!
     6 B×P+

6 N×N?! P-Q4 makes matters very comfortable for Black — after recapturing the piece he will be threatening White's QP.

     6 ...   K×B
     7 N×N   R-K1

Black's excellent pair of bishops balances the slight weakness of his backward KP.

C

1 P-K4 P-Q3 2 P-Q4 N-KB3 3 N-QB3 P-KN3 4 B-QB4 B-N2

        5 N-B3   P-B3 (*76*)

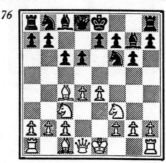

Now White's main tries are:

C1 6 O-O

C2 6 P-K5

C3 6 Q-K2

C4 6 B-N3

C1

1 P-K4 P-Q3 2 P-Q4 N-KB3 3 N-QB3 P-KN3 4 B-QB4 B-N2 5 N-B3 P-B3

        6 O-O   P-QN4!

Active play gaining space on the Q-side at the expense of White's exposed KB. 7 B-N3? loses a pawn after 7...P-N5 8 N-N1 (or 8 N-K2) 8...N×P. Feller-Keene, Siegen 1970, continued 7 B-Q3 P-N5 8 N-K2 B-N5 9 N-N3 QN-Q2 10 P-KR3 B×N and Black had an initiative on the Q-side.

C2

1 P-K4 P-Q3 2 P-Q4 N-KB3 3 N-QB3 P-KN3 4 B-QB4 B-N2 5 N-B3 P-B3

        6 P-K5   N-Q4

        7 B×N

7 N×N? P×N 8 B×P?? Q-R4+ and White loses the bishop. By moving it on the 8th turn 7 N×N? is revealed as a waste of a tempo.

        7 ...   P×B

and now, after 8 N×P Q-R4+ 9 N-B3 P×P 10 N×P B×N 11 P×B Q×KP+ 12 B-K3, Black has a comfortable position.

C3

1 P-K4 P-Q3 2 P-Q4 N-KB3 3 N-QB3 P-KN3 4 B-QB4 B-N2 5 N-B3 P-B3

6 Q-K2   O-O (77)

7 P-K5

For 7 B-N3 see C4. 7 B-KN5 P-N4 and 8 B-N3? is poor because of 8...P-QR4 with the nasty threats of...B-QR3 and...P-N5 and...P-R5. Therefore 8 B-Q3 Q-B2 intending...P-K4. 9 P-K5 crosses this plan but after 9...PxP 10 NxKP (10 PxP? N-N5 winning the KP) 10...B-K3=; Black's pieces are active and White cannot maintain his knight outpost on K5.

7 O-O P-QN4 8 B-N3 (8 B-Q3 is similar to Feller-Keene) 8...P-N5 9 N-Q1 B-QR3 10 B-QB4 BxB 11 QxB NxP 12 QxNP Q-N3∓ Lukin-Matokhin, Leningrad 1965. Black holds the centre and has the better bishop.

7 ...   PxP
8 PxP   N-Q4

9 B-Q2 NxN 10 BxN P-QN4 11 B-Q3 Q-N3 12 P-QN4 B-N5 Vesely-Marsalek, Ostrava 1960, gives Black a slight edge since White has loosened his pawns too much, or 9 B-KN5 P-KR3 10 B-Q2 P-QN4! is similar to the above.

C4

1 P-K4 P-Q3 2 P-Q4 N-KB3 3 N-QB3 P-KN3 4 B-QB4 B-N2 5 N-B3 P-B3

6 B-N3

Removing the bishop from any inopportune disturbance. 6 P-QR4? would not serve the same purpose in view of 6...P-Q4 7 PxP PxP 8 B-N3 B-N5 9 P-R3 BxN 10 QxB N-B3 11 B-K3 P-K3 12 O-O O-O 13 KR-Q1 R-B1 14 Q-K2 N-K1∓ Eliskases-Wade, Buenos Aires 1960. Black has an ideal position for he plans to control...QB5 by playing his knights

to Q3 and QR4, and White is powerless to interfere with the occupation
of the light squares on his Q-side.

	6 ...	O-O
	7 O-O	

7 Q-K2 B-N5 8 P-KR3 B×N 9 Q×B QN-Q2 is equal despite White's
two bishops, as Black's position is very flexible; or 7 P-KR3 P-QR4 8 P-
R3 (stopping 8...P-R5 9 B×RP N×P. 8 P-K5 P×P 9 N×P N-Q4 is all
right for Black too) 8...P-R5 9 B-R2 QN-Q2 10 O-O P-K4 11 B-K3 Q-
B2 leaves Black with a solid position.

	7 ...	B-N5
	8 P-KR3	B×N
	9 Q×B	QN-Q2

Now, after 10 B-K3 or 10 B-N5, or any rook move, Black can occupy
his fair share of the centre with 10...P-K4.

Storm on the Flank
1 P-K4 P-Q3 2 P-Q4 N-KB3 3 N-QB3 P-KN3

	4 B-K2	B-N2
	5 P-KR4	

A bold but somewhat artificial attempt to storm Black's K-side and
expose Black's KNP as a target.

	5 ...	P-B4! (*78*)

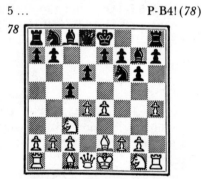

White's attempts at K-side attack are jolted by this move which
creates a fluid central position.

Now

A 6 P×P

B 6 P-Q5

A

1 P-K4 P-Q3 2 P-Q4 N-KB3 3 N-QB3 P-KN3 4 B-K2 B-N2 5 P-KR4 P-
B4!

6 P×P	Q-R4

There are now three alternatives for White:

A1 7 P×P?
A2 7 K-B1
A3 7 B-Q2

A1

1 P-K4 P-Q3 2 P-Q4 N-KB3 3 N-QB3 P-KN3 4 B-K2 B-N2 5 P-KR4 P-B4! 6 P×P Q-R4

7 P×P?	N×P
8 P×P	N×N
9 P×N	B×P+
10 K-B1	N-B3±

It is rare indeed for White to be able to answer...Q-R4 in such typical positions with P×QP and still emerge unscathed.

A2

1 P-K4 P-Q3 2 P-Q4 N-KB3 3 N-QB3 P-KN3 4 B-K2 B-N2 5 P-KR4 P-B4! 6 P×P Q-R4

7 K-B1	Q×BP
8 B-K3	Q-QR4
9 P-R5	

If 9 N-R3 B×N 10 R×B P-R4 and Black has no problems.

9 ...	P×P
10 B×KRP	

10 P-B3 likewise leads to sharp play, but this should not bother a devotee of the Pirc.

10 ...	N-B3
11 B-K2	B-K3
12 N-R3	O-O-O
13 N-B4	P-Q4!

Now Black goes over to attack with good chances; Mikenas-Gaprindasvili, Minsk 1964.

A3

1 P-K4 P-Q3 2 P-Q4 N-KB3 3 N-QB3 P-KN3 4 B-K2 B-N2 5 P-KR4 P-B4! 6 P×P Q-R4

7 B-Q2	Q×BP
8 P-R5	

8 P-QN4? is feeble, e.g. 8...Q-B2 9 R-N1 B-K3 10 P-R3 QN-Q2 11 N-N5 Q-B1 12 P-KB3 N-R4 13 K-B2 B-K4∓ Malinova-Gaprindashvili,

1957. White has no good way of defending the weak squares on the K-side.

| 8 ... | O-O |
| 9 N-R3 | B×N |

A suggestion of O'Kelly's which is still awaiting experience in tournament play.

| 10 R×B | N-B3 |

Black stands well since the white pieces are awkwardly placed and it is hard to prevent...P-Q4 breaking the position open to the advantage of the better developed side.

B

1 P-K4 P-Q3 2 P-Q4 N-KB3 3 N-QB3 P-KN3 4 B-K2 B-N2 5 P-KR3 P-B4!

6 P-Q5 (79)

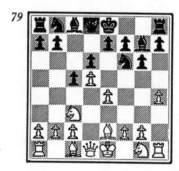

| 6 ... | O-O |
| 7 P-R5 | |

Other 7th moves give Black time to open up the central files e.g. 7 B-KN5 P-N4! 8 B×P N×KP 9 N×N Q-R4+ 10 Q-Q2 Q×B 11 P-QB3 N-Q2 12 Q-K2 Q-N3 13 N-B3 N-B3! with a strong initiative for Black, Bruzzi-Botterill 1971; or 7 N-B3 P-K3! when the move P-KR4 is just wasted and irrelevant.

| 7 ... | P-QN4 |
| 8 P×P | |

8 B×P allows the well known combination . . .N×KP!

| 8 ... | P-N5! |

An inspired sacrificial idea to wipe out White's centre.

| 9 P×RP+ | K-R1 |

The black king shelters behind his opponent's pawn.

10 N-N1	N×KP
11 N-Q2	N-KB3

White's extra pawn is worth nothing and only obstructs White's pieces in their hunt for the black king. Black has all the play in the centre. Wade-N.Littlewood, Ilford 1964, continued 12 N-B4 B-N2 13, B-B3 R-K1 14 B-R6 (trying to get at the black king) 14...B×B 15 R×B P-K3 16 P×P R×P+ 17 N-K3 N-B3 18 N-R3 Q-K2 19 Q-Q2 N-Q5 20 O-O-O N-K5 with an overwhelming position for Black.

The Classical System
1 P-K4 P-Q3 2 P-Q4 N-KB3 3 N-QB3 P-KN3

4 N-B3	B-N2
5 B-K2	

Already with his first two moves White has obtained the 'ideal' central pawn formation. He continues quiet development in the belief that this will maintain a slight edge. Black must guard against the thrust P-K5 and contest the centre at a safe moment with...P-QB4 or ...P-K4.

5 ...	O-O (80)

White now has a choice between four plausible moves:
A 6 P-KR3
B 6 B-KB4
C 6 B-KN5
D 6 O-O

A

1 P-K4 P-Q3 2 P-Q4 N-KB3 3 N-QB3 P-KN3 4 N-B3 B-N2 5 B-K2 O-O

6 P-KR3	P-K4

This move at once occupies the centre:
a) 7 P×P P×P 8 N×P N×P! and Black regains the pawn with a free game.

b) 7 P-Q5 P-QB3 with a target for counter-attack against White's central position.

B

1 P-K4 P-Q3 2 P-Q4 N-KB3 3 N-QB3 P-KN3 4 N-B3 B-N2 5 B-K2 O-O

      6 B-KB4   N-B3

      7 P-Q5

If 7 O-O then 7...B-N5 is a good move intending to force through ...P-K4 (with tempo gain because of White's bishop on KB4). Westerinen-Razuvayev, Vilnius 1969, went 7 O-O B-N5 8 P-Q5 (driving back the knight, but the advanced QP provides Black with a target for attack) 8...N-N1 9 Q-Q2 QN-Q2 10 B-KR6 B×N 11 B2×B P-B3 12 B×B K×B 13 KR-K1 Q-R4 14 P-QR3 QR-B1 15 P×P P×P 16 P-QN4 Q-B2∓ White has only succeeded in weakening his Q-side.

      7 ...   P-K4!

      8 B-KN5

Botvinnik's suggestion as an improvement on 8 P×Pep? B×P 9 O-O R-K1 10 R-K1 P-KR3 11 P-KR3 P-KN4 12 B-K3 P-Q4 13 P×P N×P 14 N×N Q×N Unzicker-Botvinnik, Varna 1962, when Black had the more active pieces — his bishops are raking White's Q-side.

      8 ...   N-K2

there could follow 9 Q-Q2 N-R4 10 O-O-O with a sharp and difficult position in which Black's prospects are not inferior.

C

1 P-K4 P-Q3 2 P-Q4 N-KB3 3 N-QB3 P-KN3 4 N-B3 B-N2 5 B-K2 O-O

      6 B-KN5   QN-Q2

A good move which prepares...P-QB4 establishing a 'Sicilian' central structure: e.g. 7 Q-Q2 P-B4 8 O-O P×P 9 N×P P-QR3 10 K-R1 Q-B2 11 P-B4 P-R3 12 B-R4 P-QN4 13 B-B3 B-N2 with equal chances, Tseshkovsky-Ushakov, USSR 1962.

D

1 P-K4 P-Q3 2 P-Q4 N-KB3 3 N-QB3 P-KN3 4 N-B3 B-N2 5 B-K2 O-O

      6 O-O   B-N5

      7 B-K3   N-B3

      8 Q-Q2

8 P-Q5 is not very impressive and merely increases the scope of Black's KB after 8...B×N 9 B×B N-K4 10 B-K2 P-B3 11 P-B4 N4-Q2 12 Q-Q2 P×P 13 P×P Q-R4 14 QR-Q1 QR-B1 15 B-Q4 N-N3 16 KR-K1 N-B5 and Black stood better, Quinones-Keene, Camaguey 1974.

      8 ...   P-K4

9 P×P

Or 9 P-Q5 N-K2 followed by a move of Black's KN (-KR4 or -K1) the retreat of Black's QB to Q2 and a K-side push with...P-KB4. In that case Black's chances on the K-side are no worse than White's on the opposite wing.

| 9 ... | P×P |
| 10 QR-Q1 | Q-B1! |

Matulovic's innovation which maintains equality while keeping some life in Black's game. Timman-Matulovic, Wijk aan Zee 1974, continued 11 Q-B1 R-Q1 12 R×R+ Q×R 13 R-Q1 Q-KB1 14 P-KR3 B×N 15 B×B P-QR3 16 N-Q5 N×N 17 R×N N-Q5 18 B×N P×B 19 Q-B4 Q-K2 20 P-K5 R-K1 21 Q×QP B×P 22 Q-Q3 B-Q3 23 P-KN3 Q-K8+ 24 K-N2 Q-QB8 25 P-N3 R-K8 26 B-Q1 ½-½. If anyone can play on it is Black whose major pieces are actively placed.

White Plays P-KB3 and B-K3
1 P-K4 P-Q3 2 P-Q4 N-KB3 3 N-QB3 P-KN3

4 P-B3

The moves P-KB3 and B-K3 indicated that White probably intends to castle long and attempt to storm the K-side with the conventional Q-Q2, B-KR6, P-KR4 etc. Black, however, has many opportunities to rebut White's attacking efforts.

4 ... P-B3

Black's best chance because it prepares to counter-attack on the Q-side where White intends to castle(...P-QN4 and...Q-R4 are both now possible).

| 5 B-K3 | QN-Q2 |
| 6 Q-Q2 | B-N2 (*81*) |

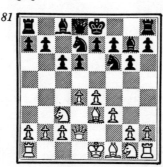

Black has furthered his development with his last two moves and is ready to withstand any of White's attacking plans. The main 7th move alternatives to 7 B-KR6 (D) are:-

A 7 O-O-O
B 7 KN-K2
C 7 P-KN4
D 7 B-KR6

A

1 P-K4 P-Q3 2 P-Q4 N-KB3 3 N-QB3 P-KN3 4 P-B3 P-B3 5 B-K3 QN-Q2 6 Q-Q2 B-N2

        7 O-O-O   Q-R4

Immediately starting an attack on White's king.

        8 K-N1   N-N3

and now if:

a) 9 N-Q5 Q×Q 10 N×N+ B×N 11 R×Q P-Q4= Blau-Medina, Zurich 1964.

b) 9 B-Q3 (a better attempt than the simplifying 9 N-Q5) 9...B-K3 10 Q-K2 N-R5 11 N×N Q×N 12 P-QN3 and Black will have to regroup for the attack.

B

1 P-K4 P-Q3 2 P-Q4 N-KB3 3 N-QB3 P-KN3 4 P-B3 P-B3 5 B-K3 QN-Q2 6 Q-Q2 B-N2

        7 KN-K2

and Black can reach a position, with even chances, as in Milic-Pirc, Belgrade 1952, with 7...N-N3 8 N-B1 B-K3 9 N-N3 N-B5 10 B×N B×B 11 B-R6 B×B 12 Q×B Q-N3.

C

1 P-K4 P-Q3 2 P-Q4 N-KB3 3 N-QB3 P-KN3 4 P-B3 P-B3 5 B-K3 QN-Q2 6 Q-Q2 B-N2

        7 P-KN4

7...P-QN4 8 P-KR4 P-KR4! (holding White's attack) 9 N-R3 N-N3 10 P-N3 P-R4 11 P-R4 P-N5 12 N-K2 N.B3-Q2 13 R-Q1 Q-B2 14 K-B2 P-QB4 where Matanovic and Pirc agreed a draw, Zagreb 1955.

D

1 P-K4 P-Q3 2 P-Q4 N-KB3 3 N-QB3 P-KN3 4 P-B3 P-B3 5 B-K3 QN-Q2 6 Q-Q2 B-N2

        7 B-KR6   B×B
        8 Q×B   P-QN4
        9 O-O-O

Other 9th moves offer White little chance of advantage e.g.:

a) 9 N-R3 P-N5 10 N-Q1 Q-N3 11 Q-Q2 P-B4 12 P×P N×BP= Bakulin-

Botvinnik, Moscow 1964. Black's KB has been exchanged but White's
pieces are passively placed. Or
b) 9 B-Q3 P-K4 10 P×P P×P 11 O-O-O Q-K2 12 KN-K2 P-R3 13 K-N1
B-N2 14 N-B1 N-B4 15 N-N3 N×N 16 RP×N O-O-O= Kupreichik-
Razuvaev, Batumi 1969. If anything Black has the more active position.

9 ...   P-N5

10 N3-K2   Q-N3

This tense situation with rival attacks underway arose in Karasev-
Averbakh, Harkov 1963, which continued 11 K-N1 P-R4 12 N-B1 P-R5
13 P-N4 P-B4 14 P×P N×BP 15 N.N1-K2 B-Q2 16 Q-K3 O-O with
chances for both sides.

11 White vs The Pirc

The Robert Byrne Variation
1 P-K4 P-Q3 2 P-Q4 N-KB3 3 N-QB3 P-KN3
4 B-KN5 (*82*)

An aggressive and natural system with an advantage over the system of development that characterises the Austrian Attack—the QB is posted on the business side of the pawn front. If White pushes P-K5 the pressure along the diagonal KR4-Q8 may become painful for Black. Also dangerous is the continuation Q-Q2 with P-KB5 in the air intending B-KR6 to exchange Black's fianchettod bishop and perhaps launch a pawn storm against the black K-side. The American grandmaster and recent world championship candidate Robert Byrne is the line's chief exponent.

Black has four reasonable replies to 4 B-KN5:

A 4...B-N2
B 4...P-KR3
C 4...P-B3
D 4...QN-Q2

A

4 ...	B-N2

Or 1 P-K4 P-KN3 2 P-Q4 B-N2 3 N-QB3 P-Q3 4 B-KN5 N-KB3

5 Q-Q2	P-KR3

5...P-B3 will normally transpose into variation C.

6 B-KB4

Now Black cannot castle on the K-side because of the pressure on his KR3 and he has a lot of developing to get through before he can castle on the Q-side.

6 ...   P-KN4

Very double edged, but alternatives are not attractive.

a) 6...P-B3 7 P-B3 N3-Q2? (7...P-QN4 is a better chance) 8 O-O-O Q-R4 9 K-N1 N-N3 10 P-K5 P-Q4 11 P-KR4 B-K3 12 N-R3 N1-Q2 13 N-QN5! Q×Q 14 N-B7+ K-B1 15 R×Q Levin-Kostuchenko, Kiev 1959. White has a tremendous advantage with possibilities of N×B and P-R5 to shut in Black's KB for ever.

b) 6...QN-Q2 7 O-O-O ±

c) 6...N-B3!? 7 B-QN5 N-Q2 8 N-B3 P-R3 9 B-K2 P-QN4? (9...P-K4 10 P×P N2×P gives Black equalizing chances) 10 O-O-O P-N4 11 B-K3 N-B3 12 P-Q5 P-QN5 13 P×N P×N 14 Q×BP O-O 15 P-K5± Veresov-Zaitsev, Moscow 1964. Black is a pawn down and his king position is weak as well.

7 B-K3

Now Bivshev-Shilov, Sochi 1961, continued 7...N-N5 8 O-O-O P-QB3 9 P-KR4 N×B 10 Q×N P-N5 11 P-B4 Q-R4 12 P-K5 P×P 13 QP×P B-K3 14 K-N1 N-Q2 15 KN-K2 N-N3 16 N-Q4 N-Q4 17 N×N Q×N 18 P-B4 Q-B4 19 Q-QB3 O-O-O 20 B-K2 B-Q2 21 P-N4 Q-N3 22 P-QB5 Q-B2 23 Q-B4 with great advantage to White—space advantage and tactical possibilities such as P-K6.

B

1 P-K4 P-Q3 2 P-Q4 N-KB3 3 N-QB3 P-KN3 4 B-KN5

4 ...   P-KR3
5 B-KB4   B-N2
6 Q-Q2

and we have transposed into variation A.

C

1 P-K4 P-Q3 2 P-Q4 N-KB3 3 N-QB3 P-KN3 4 B-KN5

        4 ...   P-B3 *(83)*

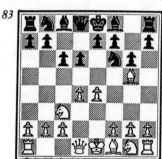

        5 P-B4   Q-N3!?

If the safer 5...B-N2, then N-B3, B-Q3 and O-O is a good plan for White.

        6 Q-Q2   Q×NP
        7 R-N1   Q-R6
        8 B-Q3

White has a big lead in development and a menacing position for a pawn.

D

1 P-K4 P-Q3 2 P-Q4 N-KB3 3 N-QB3 P-KN3 4 B-KN5

        4 ...   QN-Q2

        5 P-B4 *(84)*

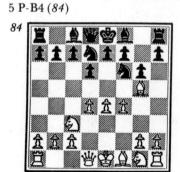

Immediately threatening P-K5. This is the only move to give White's system any bite.

        5 ...   P-KR3

Pirc used to play 5...N-N3 or 5...P-B3 here but neither move is satisfactory:

a) 5...N-N3 6 P-QR4 7 B-Q3 B-N2 8 N-B3 and now 8...O-O 9 O-O N.B3-Q2 10 Q-K1 P-KB3 11 B-R4 P-QB4 12 P-Q5, Trifunovic-Pirc, Belgrade 1952. leaves Black with weak squares and boxed in pieces; or 8...N-R4 9 P-B5! P×P 10 P×P P-R3 11 B-Q2 N-B3 12 Q-K2 P-B3 13 P-KN4 and White already had a promising attack in Djurasevic-Pirc, Belgrade 1952.

b) 5...P-B3 6 P-K5 N-Q4 7 N×N P×N 8 N-B3 Q-N3 9 B-Q3 B-N2 10 Q-K2 and now 10...P×P 11 BP×P N-B1 12 P-B3 B-Q2 13 O-O N-K3 14 QR-K1 O-O 15 B-K3 gave White a fine centralised position with chances on the K-side in Grosek-Pirc, 3rd Yugoslav Championship 1947. or 10...P-B3 11 P×BP N×P 12 B-N5+ B-Q2 13 B×N B×B.B3 14 B×B+ K×B 15 O-O-O with obvious weaknesses in Black's position, Udovcic-Pirc. 8th Yugoslav Championship 1952.

6 B-R4	N-R4!?

Introduced by Benko against Ostojic at Monaco 1969. Seemingly in violation of general principles it is. nevertheless, a subtle method of striving for control of central squares. The move prepares...B-N2 and ...P-QB4 pressurizing the dark squares and especially White's QP. And now alternatives are:

D1 7 Q-Q2
D2 7 P-B5
D3 7 KN-K2

D1

1 P-K4 P-Q3 2 P-Q4 N-KB3 3 N-QB3 P-KN3 4 B-KN5 QN-Q2 5 P-B4 P-KR3 6 B-R4 N-R4!?

7 Q-Q2	N×P!
8 Q×N	P-KN4
9 Q-B2	

9 B×P P×B 10 Q×NP B-R3 11 Q-N3 P-QB4 and Black has excellent play on the dark squares. 9 Q-B3 P×B 10 B-B4 P-K3 11 B×P N-K4 12 P×N B×B with advantage.

9 ...	P×B
10 B-B4	P-K3
11 O-O-O	N-N3
12 B-K2	B-Q2
13 N-R3	

If 13 N-B3 then ...B-K2 is possible. retaining the extra pawn.

13 ...	Q-K2
14 KR-B1	R-R2

We have been following Richardson-Keene, Paignton 1969. Black has good prospects, his bishop pair and extra pawn compensating for his cramped position.

D2

1 P-K4 P-Q3 2 P-Q4 N-KB3 3 N-QB3 P-KN3 4 B-KN5 QN-Q2 5 P-B4 P-KR3 6 B-R4 N-R4!?

       7 P-B5 (*85*)

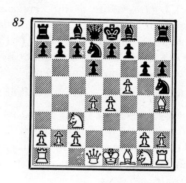

85

     7 ...   B-N2
     8 P×P

Ostoijic tried 8 B-B4 against Benko, but did not do well; 8 B-B4 N-B5 9 Q-B3? (9 Q-Q2 is better) 9...P-KN4 10 B-B2 P-B4!∓ Black has seized control of his K4 square, a common theme in this line.

     8 ...   P×P
     9 B-B4   P-B4
    10 KN-K2   N-N3
    11 B-QN5+   B-Q2
    12 O-O

12 P×P B×B 13 N×B P×P 14 O-O P-R3 with equal chances, or 12 B×B+ Q×B 13 P×P Q-N5! and the initiative is firmly in Black's hands.

    12 ...   B×B
    13 N×B   Q-Q2
    14 P-R4   P-R3
    15 N5-B3   N-QB5=

D3

1 P-K4 P-Q3 2 P-Q4 N-KB3 3 N-QB3 P-KN3 4 B-KN5 QN-Q2 5 P-B4 P-KR3 6 B-R4 N-R4!?

7 KN-K2 *(86)*

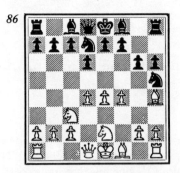

Threatening to acquire a massive position by means of P-KN4, P-KR3 and B-N2.

7 ...	P-KN4!?

a) 7...N×P? 8 N×N P-KN4 9 N-K6 P×N 10 Q-R5 mate!!
b) 7...P-QB4 8 N-Q5! and Black's pieces are painfully hemmed in.

8 P×P	P-K3

8...P-K4 9 Q-Q2 B-K2 10 O-O-O±. Black has severe weaknesses at ...Q4 and ...KB4.

9 Q-Q2	B-K2
10 O-O-O	P×P
11 B-B2	P-QB3

and both sides have chances in the struggle ahead. Black plans...P-QB4 followed by strong-pointing his K4 square.

12 Centre Counter Game (Scandinavian Defence)

1 P-K4 P-Q4

Many of the openings that were popular fifty years ago or more have disappeared almost completely from master chess. The reason for this is not merely that fashions change but that some of these older lines have been shown to be just plain bad. One such opening is the Centre Counter Game, a defence which allows White to make full use of his one move initiative.

1 P-K4	P-Q4
2 P×P	

Black may now follow one of two distinct paths:

A 2...Q×P

B 2...N-KB3

The gambit, 2...P-QB3?, sacrifices a pawn for the sake of getting a lost game: After 3 P×P N×P (or 3...P-K4 4 P×P B×P 5 P-Q3 B-B4 6 N-QB3, when White has reached a safe form of the Danish Gambit reversed in which his two extra pawns give him a two pawn advantage.) 4 P-Q3 P-K4 5 N-KB3 B-QB4 6 B-K2 N-B3 7 O-O, Black has nothing to show for his pawn.

A

1 P-K4 P-Q4 2 P×P

2 ...	Q×P (87)

This, the oldest form of the Centre Counter, gives White a lasting lead in development.

3 N-QB3	Q-QR4

3...Q-Q1 is too passive and 4 P-Q4 N-KB3 (after 4...N-QB3 5 N-B3 B-N5 P-Q5, the game Mieses-Ohquist, 1896, concluded amusingly with 6...N-K4? 7 N×N B×Q 8 B-QN5+ 1-O. Naturally this game is not an inevitable consequence of Black's fourth move but it does seem rather illogical for Black to first develop a piece that can be attacked at will.) 5 B-K3 P-B3 (not 5...N-B3? 6 P-Q5) 6 B-Q3 B-N5 7 KN-K2 P-K3 8 Q-Q2 gives White an irresistible hold on the centre and a beautifully developed game, Tarrasch-Pillsbury, 1903.

3...Q-K4+? is another time-wasting move. A postal game Koch-Mayer, 1952, continued 4 B-K2 B-N5 (if 4...P-QB3 5 N-B3 Q-B2 6 P-Q4 B-B4 7 P-Q5!±) 5 P-Q4 B×B 6 KN×B Q-KR4 7 P-Q5! Q-N5 8 Q-Q3 (threatening 9 Q-N5+) 8...P-QB3 (not 8...Q×NP?) 9 B-KB4 Q-B1 10 O-O-O and Black's 'undevelopment' presents a sorry spectacle.

4 P-Q4	P-K4

4...N-KB3 5 N-B3 B-N5 is best met by 6 P-KR3! and now:

a) 6...B×N 7 Q×B P-B3 8 B-QB4 P-K3 9 O-O QN-Q2 10 B-B4 B-K2 11 KR-K1 O-O 12 P-R3 KR-K1 13 B-KN3! Q-N3 14 Q-Q3 QR-Q1 15 P-QN4! with a tremendous game for White, Botvinnik-Konstantinopolsky, USSR 1952;

b) 6...B-R4 7 P-KN4 B-N3 8 N-K5 P-B3 (8...N-K5? 9 Q-B3!) 9 P-KR4! and Black's position bears a strong resemblance to a bad form of the Caro-Kann. 9...B-K5? is now met by 10 N-B4 Q-B2 11 N×B N×N 12 Q-B3 N-B3 13 B-B4±; 9...N-K5 by 10 B-Q2 Q-N3 (or 10...N×B 11 Q×N P-B3 12 N×B P×N 13 B-Q3 P-KN4 14 P-R5 N-Q2 15 B-N6+ with a winning position due to Black's wrecked K-side) 11 N×B N×N 12 B×N RP×N 13 Q-Q2 P-K3 14 O-O-O Q-B2 15 R-K1± (analysis by Tartakower); and 9...QN-Q2 by 10 N-B4 Q-B2 11 P-R5 B-K5 12 R-R4! (threatening to win a piece by 13 P-N5) 12...B-Q4 13 P-N5± Krasnov-Bondar, USSR 1962. Black must retreat his attacked knight as 13...B×N 14 B×B N-Q4 loses a pawn.

5 N-B3	B-KN5

The only logical continuation. 5...P×P? 6 N×P B-QN5 7 B-Q2 Q-K4+ 8 Q-K2 Q×Q+ 9 B×Q gives White an important lead in development, while 5...B-QN5 also fails to solve Black's problems: 6 B-Q2 B-N5 (6...P×P is again a mistake. Tal-Skuja, 1968, continued 7 Q-K2+ N-K2 8 N×P O-O 9 P-QR3 B-Q3 10 N4-N5 Q-N3 11 O-O-O B-K3 12 B-N5! N-N3 13 N×B P×N 14 P-KR4±) 7 P-QR3 B-Q3 (not 7...B.KN5×N 8 RP×B B×Q 9 R×Q B×P 10 R×KP+ etc.) 8 B-QB4 P×P 9

Q-K2+ Q-K4 10 Q×Q+ B×Q 11 N×B P×N 12 B×KBP+ K-K2 13 B×P B-K3 14 B×B K×B 15 O-O-O and Black's position, a pawn down with his king exposed on the central files, is hopeless.

6 P-KR3   **P×P**

6...B-R4? is an outsize blunder: 7 P-KN4! P×P (7...B-N3? 8 N×P) 8 Q×P B-N3 9 B-Q2 N-QB3 10 B-QN5 KN-K2 11 N-K5! with an overwhelming position for White.

     6...B×N 7 Q×B is also bad for Black after either 7...P-QB3 8 B-QB4 N-B3 9 O-O or 7...P×P 8 Q×NP P×N 9 P-QN3!

7 Q×P   **B×N**

8 Q-K3+   **B-K2**

9 Q×B.B3

White threatens 10 B-QB4 as well as 10 Q×NP and Black has grave difficulties completing his development. (if 9...Q-N5 10 P-QR3!).

B

1 P-K4 P-Q4 2 P×P

2 ...   N-KB3 (*88*)

3 P-Q4

It should be noted that White may, if he so wishes, transpose to Gunderam's Attack in the Caro-Kann (chapter 8) by 3 P-QB4 P-B3 4 P-Q4 P×P 5 P-B5.

3 ...   N×P

Black must recapture the pawn at once. If instead he plays 3...P-KN3?, 4 P-QB4 forces 4... P-QN4 (otherwise Black is just a pawn down) and then comes 5 P-B5! N×P 6 B×P+ P-QB3 7 B-K2, with a useful protected passed pawn at QB5 and Black is, anyway, a pawn down as well. 3...P-B3 is akin to 2...P-QB3 in that it offers a pawn for which Black gets no return: 4 P×P N×P 5 N-KB3 B-N5 6 B-K2±.

4 P-QB4   N-N3

This move gives the opening certain characteristics thar make it reminiscent of Alekhine's Defence. Black hopes to undermine White's impressive looking pawn duo at Q4 and QB4 by such means as...N-QB3...P-K4 and possibly a K-side fianchetto.

4...N-KB3 would be a passive step, allowing White to support, maintain and even augment his central control. viz: 5 N-KB3 and now: a) 5...P-B3 6 N-B3 B-N5 7 B-K3 P-K3 8 B-K2!± (Fine); b) 5...B-N5 6 B-K2 P-K3 7 Q-N3 Q-B1 8 N-B3 and White has the advantage since he controls more spaces; or c) 5...P-KN3 6 N-B3 B-N2 7 P-KR3 O-O 8 B-K3, and White can continue with Q-Q2, B-K2 and R-Q1 with an enormous grip on the centre.

4...N-N5? is just plain wrong—its only justification would come if White overlooked the threat of 5...Q×P 6 Q×Q N-B7+ winning a pawn for nothing. After 5 P-QR3! N5-B3 6 P-Q5 N-K4 7 N-KB3 N×N+ (7...B-N5 8 Q-N3!) 8 Q×N, Black has exchanged off a piece that has already moved five times for one that had only moved once. White's game is clearly superior.

5 N-KB3   B-N5

The only active continuation—Black at once applies indirect pressure to White's QP.

5...P-N3 is a little slow; White has ample time with which to contest the long diagonal by 6 B-Q2 B-N2 7 B-B3. Mardle-Hollis, 1962, continued 7...O-O 8 B-K2 B-N5 9 O-O B×N 10 B×B N-B3 11 P-Q5 N-K4 12 B-K2 and once again White has a greater share of the board. Note that 12...N (either)×BP loses a piece after 13 B×B, 14 B×N and 15 Q-Q4+.

6 P-B5!

This, the key to White's whole system, was discovered by the Soviet theoritician grandmaster Suetin, and first employed in master practice by him in his game with Shamkovich from the 1965 USSR Championship. The idea is to take advantage of Black's voluntary weakening of his QN2 square and thereby to unpin White's KN.

6 ...   B×N

6...N-Q4 allows White to put into practice the full force of Suetin's argument. After 7 Q-N3! B×N 8 Q×P N-K6 9 Q×B N-B7+ 10 K-Q1 N×R 11 Q×R, White's material advantage is overwhelming. 7...N-QB3 is a marked improvement (over 7...B×N) but White can safely snatch the QNP: 8 Q×P N4-N5 9 B-QN5 B-Q2 10 B×N N×B 11 Q-N3 and Black has no compensation for the pawn.

6...N3-Q2 is a move that was tried by Karaklajic shortly after the Suetin-Shamkovich game. Karaklajic has long been a supporter of the Centre Counter and has contributed much to the theory of the defence. In this case, however, although his move does rank as an improvement over the text, it still fails to provide Black with sufficient resources. After simply 7 B-K2, White has a good game.

7 Q×B	N-Q4
8 Q-QN3!	P-QN3

Since 8...N-QB3 9 Q×P N4-N5 loses at once to 10 B-QN5.

        9 B-KN5

Now White threatens 10 B-QB4 P-QB3 11 N-B3 winning at least a pawn.

9 ...	Q-Q2

Not 9...P-KR3 10 B-QB4 which wins because of the second degree threat of B×BP+ K-Q2, Q-K6 mate.

10 N-B3	P-K3

10...N×N 11 P×N P-K3 would be slightly better but Black's position would still be under tremendous pressure.

11 N×N	Q×N

Or 11...P×N, 12 P-B6! imposes a similar bind to the one in the game (12...Q×BP?? 13 B-N5).

12 Q×Q	P×Q
13 P-B6!	

A beautiful move which leaves Black's Q-side completely bottled up. The pawn cannot be captured because of (13...N×P??) 14 B-N5 K-Q2 15 R-QB1 and Black can resign.

Now White's game plays itself. The Suetin-Shamkovich game concluded 13...B-K2 14 B-K3 K-Q1 15 R-B1 R-K1 16 P-KN3 B-N4 17 B-N2! B×B 18 P×B R×P+ 19 K-Q2 R-K3 20 KR-B1 P-B3 21 R-B5 R-Q3 22 R×QP R×R 23 B×R K-K2 24 B-N2 N-R3 25 P-QR3 (leaving Black's knight miserably confined) 25... R-Q1 26 R-K1+ K-Q3 27 P-QN4 (suddenly placing Black's king in a mating net) 27...P-QN4 28 P-Q5 N-B4 29 P×N+ K×P.B4 30 R-K7 1-0.

13 Nimzowitsch's Defence

1 P-K4 N-QB3

One of the features that characterised Nimzowitsch's play was his penchant for trying to control the centre with pieces rather than pawns. The defence named after him conforms to this principle from the outset. Its unnatural looking first move is no cause for jest — the defence does offer White a slight but definite advantage yet it would be most unwise to take it too lightly and try for a quick crush. The strategy that we recommend for White leads to a French Defence type of position in which Black's...N-QB3 prohibits the tematic freeing move...P-QB4.

1 P-K4	N-QB3
2 P-Q4	P-Q4(89)

The most incisive reply, though there are naturally other moves that deserve attention.

a) 2...P-K3 3 N-KB3 P-Q4 4 P-K5 P-QN3 (Cording-Braune, postal game 1965, went instead 4...P-B3 5 B-QN5 B-Q2 6 Q-K2 Q-K2 7 O-O O-O-O 8 R-K1 R-K1 9 P-B3 with some advantage since White has retained control of K5 and can advance his pawns against Black's king) 5 P-B3 N3-K2 (or 5...B-N2 6 B-Q3 P-B4 7 P×Pep Q×P 8 O-O P-KR3 9 R-K1 and here too White's control of K5 gives him the edge — Naglis-Bonch-Osmolovsky, 1960) 6 B-Q3 P-QR3 7 Q-K2± White has much more freedom of action and Black lacks development.

b) 2...P-K4 3 P×P N×P 4 N-KB3 Q-B3 (or 4...B-N5+ 5 P-B3 B-Q3 6 N-Q4 ±) 5 B-K2 B-N5+ 6 QN-Q2 N×N+ 7 B×N N-K2 8 O-O O-O 9 N-N3 shows Black's KB to be misplaced, Keres-Kevitz, 1954.

c) 2...P-Q3 3 P-Q5 N-N1 (after 3...N-K4 4 N-QB3 P-QB4 5 P-B4 N-Q2 6 N-B3 P-KN3 White's strong pawn centre is very dangerous. e.g. 7 P-K5 B-N2 8 P-K6 P×P 9 P×P N-N1 10 P-B5! N-KB3 11 N-KN5 P×P 12 B-Q3± Bogdanovic-Nikolic, Vrnajcka Banja, 1965) 4 N-K2 P-K4 5 P×Pep B×P 6 QN-B3 N-QB3 7 N-B4 Q-Q2 8 B-K2 N-B3 9 O-O O-O-O 10 N4-Q5 B-K2 11 P-QN4! N-QN1 12 B-K3 when White has considerable attacking chances, Konig-Mieses, 1939.

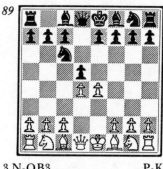

3 N-QB3   P-K3

On 3...P×P, Czerniak's suggestion 4 P-Q5! is very strong, Black's knight being faced with an unfortunate dilemma. e.g. 4...N-K4 5 P-B3! (a promising gambit) 5...P×P (or 5...P-K3 6 Q-Q4±) 6 N×P N×N+ 7 Q×N N-B3 8 B-KB4 P-QR3 9 P-KR3 P-KN3 10 P-KN4 B-N2 11 O-O-O O-O 12 Q-N3 with a tremendous position for the pawn, Mestrovic-Nikolic, Vrnajcka Banja, 1965; or 4...N-N1 5 B-KB4 N-KB3 6 B-B4 P-KN3 7 Q-K2 B-B4 8 O-O-O B-N2 9 P-B3 P×P 10 N×P±. White's superior development and hold on the central squares provide ample compensation for a pawn.

4 P-K5   P-B3

Typical Nimzowitsich, hoping to smash White's influential pawn centre. Black's only plausible alternative is 4...KN-K2 which soon lands him with an unwieldy piece deployment. After 5 N3-K2 N-B4 6 N-KB3 P-QN3 7 N-B4 (±), Black's position resembles a bastardized French Defence in which there is not the usual counterplay based on the move ...P-QB4.

5 P×P   N×BP
6 N-B3   B-Q3
7 B-KN5   O-O

Or 7...B-Q2 8 Q-Q2!±

8 B-Q3   B-Q2
9 Q-Q2   Q-K1
10 O-O-O   Q-R4
11 QR-K1±

White has the more active position and some useful pressure along the K-file.

14 Benko Gambit

1 P-Q4 N-KB3 2 P-QB4 P-B4 3 P-Q5 P-QN4

Tactical players sometimes feel at a loss when meeting 1 P-Q4. The positional lines that White can choose when playing against the King's Indian and Benoni Defences are usually not to the taste of the attacking player, and all sharper defensive systems are considered theoretically dubious. All, that is, except the Benko Gambit.

During the late 1950s and early 60s the Gambit was seen from time to time in master chess but it eventually went out of fashion. A decade later it has been revived by Grandmasters Benko and Browne, and others who have witnessed their successes with the defence have jumped on the bandwagon.

The Benko Gambit is an ideal weapon for the repertoire player. Its thematic ideas are easy to understand and the same moves appear in many of its variations thereby making the Gambit relatively easy to learn. Black sacrifices a pawn on the Q-side in order to create active play for his forces which immediately set about applying pressure to White's Q-side pawns. Black's rooks work well side by side at QR1 and QN1 or they may be doubled on one file or the other depending on which white pawn is the immediate target. Black's queen can sortie out to ...QR4 or ...QN3, or it can sit at ...QB2 ready to support the eventual advance of the QBP. His QN usually makes its way via ...QR3 either to ...QB2 followed by ...QN4 or to ...QN5 followed possibly by ...Q6 (from where it can be supported by ...P-QB5). The other knight can be transferred to ...Q2 (from where it can go to ...K4 or ...QN3) and its movement opens up the long diagonal for Black's KB. In short, all of Black's pieces are used in the Q-side attack and experience suggests that Black has ample compensation for the sacrificed pawn. If Black can win White's QNP or QRP he will nearly always win the game because the remaining Q-side pawn will be isolated and exposed and his own QBP will become a strong force in the endgame.

1 P-Q4	N-KB3
2 P-QB4	

White has a variety of unusual alternatives at his disposal, none of which offers Black a serious threat. We shall content ourselves with giving a brief mention of one active idea each against some of the alternatives:

a) 2 N-QB3 P-Q4 3 B-N5 (3 B-B4 is innocuous) 3...P-KR3! 4 B×N (or 4 B-R4 P-K3 5 P-K3 P-B4!) 4...KP×B 5 P-K3 P-B3 6 B-Q3 B-Q3 7 Q-B3 O-O 8 N-K2 R-K1 9 O-O-O P-QN4 10 P-KN4 P-N5 11 N-R4 N-Q2 12 P-KR4 N-N3 leaves White in a quandary, Tal-Geller, Curacao 1962.

b) 2 B-N5 N-K5 3 B-B4 (or 3 B-R4 P-Q4 4 P-KB3 N-Q3=) 3...P⁺Q4 4 P-KB3 N-KB3 5 N-B3 P-K3 6 B-N5 B-K2 7 N-R3 P-QN3 8 N-B2 B-R3 =White's pieces are not well placed to meet Black's French set-up.

c) 2 P-KB3 P-Q4 3 P-K4 P×P 4 N-B3 P×P 5 N×P (5 Q×P P-KN3 6 B-Q3 B-N2 also leaves White lacking in compensation) 5...P-KN3 6 B-QB4 B-N2 and White's gambit has only its spirit to compensate for the sacrificed pawn.

d) 2 N-KB3 P-B4 3 P-Q5 P-QN4 4 P-B4 B-N2 transposes to the Benko Gambit Declined (see page XX).

2 ...   P-B4 (90)

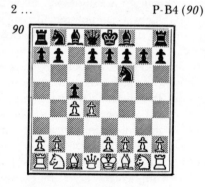

90

3 P-Q5

3 N-KB3 transposes to a line of the English Opening which may, if Black is not careful, transpose to a Sicilian Defence in which White has already established a Maroczy Bind. An interesting and virile counter to 3 N-KB3, is 3...P×P 4 N×P P-K4! e.g. 5 N-N5 (5 N-B2 P-Q4 produces a completely level position) 5...B-B4 6 N-Q6+ (not 6 N1-B3 P-Q3 7 B-N5 P-QR3 8 B×N P×B 9 Q-R4? N-B3 10 N-Q5, because of 10...P×N! 11 Q×R O-O 12 P×P N-N5 with an excellent game.) 6...K-K2 7 N×B+ (After 7 N-B5+K-B1, Black will follow up with...P-Q4 and emerge with the advantage.)

7...Q×N and now:

a) 8 N-B3 P-Q3 9 P-K3 R-Q1 10 B-K2 N-B3 11 O-O K-B1 12 P-QR3 P-QR3 (better than 12...P-QR4 giving White QN5) 13 Q-B2 N-K2 14 B-

Q2 Q-K3 15 QR-Q1 QR-B1 and Black has no problems, Konstantinopolsky-Taimanov, USSR 1948;

b) 8 B-N5 Q-B3! 9 N-B3 B-N5 10 Q-N3 N-R3 11 O-O-O B×N 12 Q×B P-Q3 13 P-K3 N-B4 14 P-B3 N-K3= Rabar-Czerniak, Belgrade 1954; White's king is no better off on the Q-side than Black's in the centre.

c) 8 P-K3 R-Q1 9 N-B3 B-N5 10 B-Q2 B×N 11 B×B N-B3 12 Q-N3 N-K5=.

3 P×P P-K4 gives Black the initiative, e.g. 4 N-QB3 (not 4 P-QN4? P-QN3! 5 P×P B×P+ 6 B-Q2 Q×P∓) 4...B×P 5 P-K4 P-KR3 6 B-Q3 P-Q3 7 P-KR3?! (better would be the immediate 7 N-B3∓) 7...N-B3 8 N-B3 B-K3 9 O-O Q-Q2! 10 P-QR3?? B×KRP! 11 P×B Q×P 12 N-KR2 N-Q5 13 B-K3 P-KR4 14 P-B3 N-N5 15 N×N Q-N6+ 0-1 Gronberg-Domino, Berlin 1956.

3 P-K3 is innocuous—after 3...P-KN3 4 N-QB3 B-N2 5 N-B3 O-O Black has an easy game.

3 ...   P-QN4 *(91)*

Part One: The Gambit Accepted

4 P×P   P-QR3

Again we have a dichotomy.

A 5 P×P

B 5 P-K3 (and other fifth moves)

A

1 P-Q4 N-KB3 2 P-QB4 P-B4 3 P-Q5 P-QN4 4 P×P P-QR3

5 P×P   B×P

6 N-QB3

6 P-KN3 P-Q3 7 B-N2 was tried in the game Ruderfer-Alburt, USSR Championship semi-final 1971. White's intention was not merely to delay the move N-QB3 but to develop his QN on Q2 and contest the long dark-squared diagonal with his bishop. The game continued: 7...P-N3 8 P-N3 B-KN2 9 B-N2 QN-Q2 10 N-Q2 O-O 11 P-K4 Q-R4 12 Q-B2, and now Black found the surprising move 12...P-B5! After 13

P×P KR-B1 14 B-QB3 Q-B4 15 R-B1 N-N5 16 N-R3 N2-K4 17 B-B1 N-K6!! 18 P×N Q×KP+, the complications eventually resulted in a draw.

6 ...   P-Q3

We now divide our survey into four main lines:

A1 7 P-K4 B×B 8 K×B
A2 7 N-B3 P-N3 8 P-K4
A3 7 N-B3 P-N3 8 N-Q2
A4 7 P-KN3 P-N3 8 B-N2

A1

1 P-Q4 N-KB3 2 P-QB4 P-B4 3 P-Q5 P-QN4 4 P×P P-QR3 5 P×P B×P
6 N-QB3 P-Q3

7 P-K4   B×B
8 K×B*(92)*

As a price for achieving the exchange of bishops White has given up his right to castle. He intends to bring his king to safety by P-KN3 followed by K-N2 but meanwhile Black can put this time to good use; continuing with his development and his preparations for a Q-side attack.

8 ...   P-N3
9 P-KN3

9 P-KN4?! is a desperate attempt that has been seen occasionally. White's idea is not only to create a 'safe' square for his king but also to try for a spatial advantage on the K-side. Black should proceed normally with 9...B-N2 and now:

a) 10 K-N2 O-O 11 P-KR3 P-K3 (with White's king exposed Black can safely open up the centre a little) 12 P×P P×P 13 P-K5 N-K1 14 P×P N×P 15 Q-K2 Q-Q2 16 P-B4 N-B3 17 N-B3 N-Q5 18 N×N P×N 19 N-K4 Q-B3 20 R-K1 KR-Q1 21 Q-B3 N×N 22 R×N P-Q6 with the better practical chances for Black, Avram-Benko, US Open Championship 1968;

b) 10 P-B3 O-O 11 KN-K2 P-K3 12 K-N2 P×P 13 N×P N-B3 14 N2-B3

NxN 15 PxN N-N5! 16 P-KR4 P-B4 17 P-N5? P-QB5 18 P-R3 N-Q6 19 R-QN1 Q-N3 20 Q-B2 KR-K1 0-1 (if 21 Q-Q2 BxN etc., or 21 K-N3 B-K4+ 22 K-N2 BxN 23 PxB Q-B4) Visier-Benko, Malaga 1969.

9 KN-K2 B-N2 10 N-B4 O-O 11 P-KN4 is a somewhat stronger idea which was successful in Formanek-Browne, Atlantic Open 1970. The difference between this and the previous move is that with his knight on KB4 White prevents . . .P-K3 and can continue with his K-side attack without fear of retaliation in the centre. Or can he? After 11...N-R3 12 P-KR4, Black should not continue as Browne did (12...Q-R4?) but with 12...Q-B1! e.g. 13 P-N5 N-KN5 (threatening 14...B-Q5) 14 N3-K2 R-N1 with good play for the pawn.

9	...	B-N2
10	K-N2	O-O
11	KN-K2	Q-N3
12	R-QN1	

So as to be able to develop his QB.

12	...	N-R3
13	P-N3	N-B2
14	P-B3	P-K3!

While White is overprotecting his whole army Black strikes out in the centre. The move . . .P-K3 is sometimes a strategic error in the Benko Gambit because it opens up a file which can be used by White to force the exchange of some of the heavy pieces. When White's king is a little exposed however, the opening up of the position is usually to Black's advantage.

15	PxP

15 B-K3 at once has been suggested as an improvement, but after 15...PxP 16 PxP KR-K1! Black has a fine game (17 B-B2 Q-N2!)

15	...	PxP
16	B-K3	Q-B3
17	Q-Q2?	

Correct would have been 17 P-QN4 PxP 18 RxP KR-N1 19 Q-N3 N-Q2, with play on the Q-side files providing sufficient compensation for the pawn.

Now Black is on top.

17	...	P-Q4
18	PxP	PxP
19	B-B4	P-Q5∓

Gross-Benko, US Open Championship 1968.

A2

1 P-Q4 N-KB3 2 P-QB4 P-B4 3 P-Q5 P-QN4 4 P×P P-QR3 5 P×P B×P
6 N-QB3 P-Q3

	7 N-B3	P-N3
	8 P-K4(*93*)	

93

	8 ...	B×B
	9 K×B	B-N2
	10 P-KN3	

Gligoric has suggested 10 P-KR3 O-O 11 K-N1 so as to use the square KR2 instead of KN2 for his king. This idea was tested in the game Hort-Jimenez, Palma Interzonal 1970: 11...QN-Q2 12 K-R2 Q-R4 13 R-K1 KR-N1 14 R-K2 N-K1 15 R-B2 N-B2 16 B-Q2 N-N4. While White has carried out a tortuous consolidating manoeuvre Black has been busy mobilising his whole army. Black's game is by far the more active and were the difference in playing strengths not so enormous he would surely have converted his advantage into a win.

Another possibility which seems even more convincing is Parma's 11...N-R3! 12 K-R2 Q-N3 which he tried in his game with Schaufelberger at Luxemburg 1971. Play continued 13 N-Q2 N-Q2 14 Q-K2 N-N5 15 N-B4 Q-R3 16 R-K1 N-K4 17 N×N B×N+ 18 P-KN3 KR-N1 19 Q×Q R×Q 20 R-K2 N-Q6 21 R-Q2 N-K8∓.

	10 ...	O-O
	11 K-N2	QN-Q2

A flexible move, reserving the option of . . .Q-N3 or . . .Q-R4.

| | 12 R-K1 | Q-R4 |

12...N-N5 13 P-KR3 N5-K4 is also good enough to maintain the balance. Trifunovic-Kozomara, Yugoslav Championship 1963, continued 14 N×N N×N 15 P-B4 N-Q2 16 Q-Q2 Q-N3 with a roughly even position.

	13 B-N5	P-R3
	14 B×N	

According to Browne, 14 B-K3 and 14 B-B4 can both be answered by
14...N-N5 with a good game for Black in each case.

14	...	B×B
15	Q-Q3?!	

15 Q-Q2 is better, gaining a tempo by attacking the KRP. Even so,
Black's initiative (after 15...K-N2) is still significant. White's QNP will
come under renewed pressure after . . .KR-N1, . . .R-N2 and . . .QR-
N1, and now that White has no dark squared bishop he will forever
have problems along the long diagonal.

15	...	KR-N1
16	R-K2?!	

And here 16 QR-N1 is better according to Browne, though White
would still be on the defensive. Now comes a combination that
frequently occurs in the Benko Gambit.

16	...	R×P!
17	R×R	Q×N
18	Q×Q	B×Q
19	R1-QN1	B×R
20	R×B	R-R5!

Black has regained his pawn and now has two typical advantages on
which to base his winning plan: (1) White's QRP is isolated and weak,
and (2) Black's QBP is strong, passed and protected.

P. Parr-Browne, Adelaide 1971, continued 21 P-K5 (if 21 N-Q2 N-
K4 22 K-B1 N-Q6 23 R-N7 K-B1 followed by . . .N-B8 or . . .N-N5
winning the RP) 21...N×P 22 N×N P×N and Black was winning the
rook ending.

A3
1 P-Q4 N-KB3 2 P-QB4 P-B4 3 P-Q5 P-QN4 4 P×P P-QR3 5 P×P B×P
6 N-QB3 P-Q3

7	N-B3	P-N3
8	N-Q2(94)	

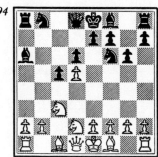

The idea of White's manoeuvre is to be able to recapture with the knight after P-K4 B×B.

8	...	B-KN2
9	P-K4	B×B
10	N×B	O-O
11	N-K3	Q-R4
12	O-O	Q-R3!

Now that the light squared bishops have been exchanged Black can captalize on White's weaknesses on the f1:a6 diagonal. In particular, White's Q3 square is rather vulnerable.

    13   B-Q2

If 13 Q-B2 QN-Q2 14 P-B3 (not 14 P-QN3? N×KP) 14...N-N3 15 P-QN3 N.B3-Q2 16 B-N2 KR-B1! with good play for the pawn. Black is preparing for . . .P-B5.

13	...	QN-Q2
14	P-QN3	

Spassov-Tringov, Varna 1973, went 14 Q-B2 P-B5! 15 N-K2 N-B4 16 N-N3 KR-B1 17 B-B3 Q-R5 with equal chances. The text is an attempt to prevent . . .P-B5.

    14   ...   Q-Q6!

Interfering with the regrouping of White's minor pieces.

15	Q-B2	N-K4
16	QR-N1	KR-N1
17	P-B3	N-K1
18	KR-Q1	N-B2
19	Q×Q	N×Q
20	K-B1	R-N2
21	P-N3!	

The only move (believe it or not). If, for example, 21 N-B4 then 21...N-N5 22 P-QR4 N-B7 and Black's active piece play is worth much more than the pawn.

21	...	B-Q5
22	K-K2	N-N5

The chances are equal, Vilela-Levy, Camaguey 1974.

A4

1 P-Q4 N-KB3 2 P-QB4 P-B4 3 P-Q5 P-QN4 4 P×P P-QR3 5 P×P B×P 6 N-QB3 P-Q3

7 P-KN3	P-N3
8 B-N2(*95*)	

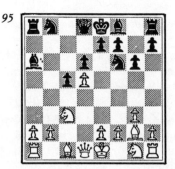

95

8 ...	B-KN2
9 N-B3	

9 N-R3 has been tried here but it looks too artificial to be of any real value—it is even difficult to find a plausible reason for the move since the logical follow-up, N-B4, achieves nothing. After the natural 9...O-O 10 O-O QN-Q2, three plans have been tested:

a) 11 N-B4 Q-B2 12 Q-B2 KR-N1 13 R-N1 P-B5 14 N-R3 N-B4 15 N-KN5 B-QB1 16 P-B3 N-R5, and Black has ample compensation for the pawn. Yanofsky-Gheorghiu, Siegen Olympiad 1970, continued 17 N×N Q-R2+ 18 K-R1 Q×N 19 P-N3 Q×RP 20 R-N2 P×P! 21 R×Q P×Q 22 R×P P-R3 23 N-R3 N×P 24 N-B4 N-N5 25 R-B7 P-K4 and Black went on to win.

b) 11 Q-B2 Q-R4 12 B-N5 KR-N1 13 KR-K1 R-R2 14 QR-N1 R2-N2 15 B-Q2 P-B5 16 P-QN4 P×Pep 17 R×P B-B5 18 R×R R×R 19 N-KN5 Q-R3 20 R-QB1 R-N1 21 B-R3. So far we have been following Denker-Benko, US Open Championship 1969. Now, with 21...N-N3!, Black could maintain his pressure and remain with a slight advantage.

c) 11 B-Q2 Q-N3 12 R-N1 KR-N1 13 P-N3 N-K1 14 Q-B2 N-B2 15 P-QR4 N-B3 16 N-B4 R-R2 17 P-QN4 P×P 18 B-K3 Q-N2 19 N-N5 B×N 20 B×R Q×B 21 P×B R×P with a slight advantage to Black. Antoshin-Mihaljicsin, Sarajevo 1970.

9 Q-R4+!? QN-Q2 10 Q-R4 is a strange idea, hoping to be able to build up a direct attack against Black's K-side. This early sortie puts White's queen offside for long enough for Black to be able to get moving on the Q-side. After 10...P-R3! 11 P-B4 R-QN1 12 P-K3 Q-R4 13 KN-K2 B-Q6! Black's game is already looking good. Barlay-Benko, USA 1968, continued 14 K-B2 P-N4 15 P×P P×P 16 Q-R4 (if 16 Q×P B-KR3!) 16...Q×Q 17 N×Q N-N5+ 18 K-K1 N×RP and Black was well on the way to victory.

9 ...	O-O
10 O-O	QN-Q2
11 Q-B2	

White has tried two alternative (though similar) plans to bolster his Q-side:

a) 11 R-N1 Q-N3 12 B-Q2 B-B5 13 P-N3 B×QP 14 N×B N×N 15 B-N5 P-K3, and Black, having won back his pawn, now enjoys a distinct advantage; Johansson-Westerinen, Dresden 1969;

b) 11 R-K1 Q-B2 12 B-Q2 (better than 12 Q-B2 KR-N1 13 B-B1? Q-B1 14 P-K4 N-N5 15 B×B Q×B 16 B-B4 N5-K4 17 N×N N×N 18 B×N B×B ∓ when White's position contains too many weak squares, Trikaliotis-Toran, Siegen Olympiad 1970) 12...N-N3 13 B-B4 KR-N1 14 P-N3 N-N5 15 B-Q2 N-B1 16 P-KR3 N-K4 17 N×N B×N 18 R-N1 N-R2 19 Q-B2 P-B5 20 R.K1-QB1 R-QB1 with roughly equal chances, Spassky-Szabo, Goteborg 1971.

11	...	Q-R4
12	R-N1	KR-QN1
13	B-Q2	N-N3?!

According to Browne, 13...N-K1, 13...R-N2 and 13...R-R2 are all superior alternatives.

14	P-N3	Q-R6
15	B-B1	Q-R4
16	B-Q2	Q-R6
17	B-B1	½-½

Padevsky-Browne, Sarajevo 1970.

B

1 P-Q4 N-KB3 2 P-QB4 P-B4 3 P-Q5 P-QN4 4 P×P P-QR3

5 P-K3(*96*)

This quiet move is unthematic in Benoni type positions because the pawn is required at K4, both to overprotect the QP and in readiness for the advance P-K5. Before we examine this move in depth, there are two others that can be mentioned:

a) 5 N-QB3?! P×P 6 N×P (not 6 P-K4? P-N5 7 P-K5 P×N 8 P×N BP×P 9 B×P Q-R4+ 10 Q-Q2 Q×Q+ 11 K×Q NP×P 12 N-B3 B-KR3+ ∓) 6... B-R3 7 N-QB3 P-Q3 and Black has gained a tempo over all of the main lines already discussed, Lorinczi-Browne, Siegen Olympiad 1970;

b) 5 P-N6 Q×P 6 N-QB3 P-N3 7 N-B3 P-Q3 8 N-Q2 (The immediate 8 P-K4 was no more successful in Sokolov-Mihaljcisin, Yugoslav Championship 1961. After 8...B-KN2 9 B-K2 O-O 10 N-Q2 P-QR4 11 N-B4 Q-R2 12 O-O B-QR3 13 P-QR4 B×N 14 B×B N-R3 15 P-B4 N-Q2 16 K-R1 N-N3 17 B-N5 N-N5 18 B-K3 Q-B2, Black's fine Q-side play gave him the advantage.) 8...B-KN2 9 P-K4 O-O 10 N-B4 Q-B2 11 B-K2 QN-Q2 12 B-B4 N-N3 13 N-K3 P-QR4 14 Q-B2 P-R5 15 O-O B-

QR3 16 B×B R×B 17 P-KR3 N.B3-Q2 18 B-N5 R-K1 (∓) 19 K-R1 P-B5 (Black has fine pressure on the Q-side without being a pawn down.) 20 QR-K1 P-R6! 21 P×P N-B4 22 N-N5 Q-Q2 23 R-QN1 P-R3 24 B-B4 N-Q6 25 B-N3 R-QB1 26 N×BP N-N7! (winning the exchange) 27 R×N R×N 28 Q-K2 B×R and Black won quickly in Adgamus-Gheorghiu, Buenos Aires 1970.

96

5 ...	P-N3
6 N-QB3	P-Q3
7 B-B4	

Played with the idea of developing the KN at K2. Three other moves come into serious consideration:

a) 7 P-N6?! (When Black has so many positional advantages to compensate for the pawn that he offers up for sacrifice, it seems rather generous of White not to accept the pawn. 'The refutation of a gambit lies in its acceptance'.) 7...QN-Q2 8 P-QR4 Q×P 9 P-R5. So far we have been following Reshevsky-Browne, Skopje 1970. Now Browne recommends 9...Q-N2 as best although in the game he got a slight advantage after 9...Q-B2 10 N-B3 B-KN2 11 P-R3 O-O 12 B-B4 R-N1 13 O-O N-K1 14 Q-K2 Q-N2 (hence Browne's preference for the immediate 9...Q-N2) 15 B-Q2 N-B2 16 Q-Q3 N-K4±; White has no compensation for Black's pressure along the QN-file;

b) 7 N-B3 B-KN2 8 B-K2 O-O 9 O-O P×P 10 B×P B-QR3 11 B×B R×B 12 Q-K2 Q-R4 13 N-Q2 QN-Q2 14 N-B4 Q-B2 15 P-K4 R1-R1 16 R-N1 N-N3 17 P-QR3 (so far as in Erwich-Lundvall, Wijk aan Zee 1970) 17...N×N with a roughly equal position;

c). 7 P×P B-KN2 8 B-N5+ (8 N-B3 O-O 9 P-K4 produces a position in which White is a tempo down on variations A1, A2 and A3.) 8...N3-Q2 9 KN-K2 O-O 10 O-O N×P 11 P-K4 N-B2 12 B-Q3 N-K4. This position offers many possibilities for both sides. Black has the usual dynamic possibilities to offset his material deficit and the practical chances are about even. Kuijpers-Benko, Wijk aan Zee 1970.

7 ...		B-KN2
8 KN-K2		O-O
9 O-O		QN-Q2
10 P×P		N-N3

White's plan of developing his bishop at QB4 is now meeting with its consequences – Black is gaining time for his Q-side attack.

11	B-N5	B×P
12	B-B6?!	

Better is 12 B×B R×B when Black will follow up with . . .Q-R1 and . . .R-N1 with good compensation for the pawn. Now White's bishop is left with nothing to do while Black's exerts its influence along the QR3-KB8 diagonal.

12	...	R-N1
13	R-N1	N-N5!

Threatening to come to K4 followed by . . .N×B and the capture of White's pawn at QB6.

14	P-B4	

Unwieldy but possibly best.

14 ...		B.N2×N!

It is most unusual for Black to give up his fianchettoed KB for White's knight at QB3. Here however, the exchange is not positionally detrimental because there is no way that White can take advantage of the weakening of the dark squares around Black's King – his QB is hemmed in on one side by the pawns at K3 and KB4 and on the other by Black's next move.

15 P×B		N-B5

Black has a beautiful position to compensate for the sacrificed pawn. Blumin-Benko, Atlantic Open 1969, concluded 16 R×R Q×R 17 Q-R4 Q-N3 18 P-K4 N-Q7 19 R-Q1 B×N 20 R×N P-B5+ 21 R-Q4 Q-N8 22 Q-R3 R-N1 23 P-R3 N-K6 24 B-R4 B-Q6 (24...R-R1 is also very strong) 25 K-B2 N-B7 26 B×N Q×B.7+ 27 K-N3 Q-K7 28 P-B5 B×P 29 R-Q2 Q-K6+ 30 K-R2 Q-B5+ 31 K-N1 R-N8 32 R-Q1 Q-N6 33 R-Q2 Q-K8+ 0-1.

The reader will appreciate, from this example, the usefulness of the QN-file as a line of infiltration.

Part Two: The Benko Gambit Declined
1 P-Q4 N-KB3 2 P-QB4 P-B4 3 P-Q5 P-QN4
4 N-KB3 (*97*)

There are a host of even more insipid moves with which White can refuse to take up the challenge:

a) 4 P-KN3 P×P 5 B-N2 P-N3 6 N-QB3 B-QN2 7 N-B3 B-N2 8 O-O O-O 9 N-K5 P-Q3 10 N×QBP QN-Q2 11 R-K1 B-QR3 and Black's game is already looking promising. Johanessen-Fischer, Havana Olympiad 1966, concluded 12 Q-R4 Q-B1 13 N-R5 N-N3 14 Q-R4 R-K1 15 B-N5 Q-B2 16 N-B6 B-N2 17 P-K4 N.N3-Q2 18 P-B4 K-R1 19 P-K5 P×P 20 P×P N×QP 21 N×N Q×N 22 P-K6?! N-K4! 23 R×N B×R 24 P×P R-KB1 25 P-KR3? (if 25 N-B4 Q-N3 26 B×B P-B5+!∓) 25...R×P 26 N-B4 R×N! 0-1.

b) 4 N-QR3 was played in Velimirovic-Negovan, Yugoslavia 1966, and now instead of 4...P-N5 congealing the Q-side, I recommend 4...P×P 5 N×P B-R3 6 P-K3 P-Q3 when Black can continue with ...QN-Q2 and an eventual ...N-N3.

c) 4 P-B3 P×P 5 P-K4 P-Q3 6 B×P P-N3 7 N-B3 B-KN2 8 KN-K2 O-O 9 O-O QN-Q2 10 B-K3 N-K4 11 B-N3 B-QR3! Lim-Browne, 'National Open' 1971, and Black's control of ...Q6 gives him a clear advantage.

d) 4 P-QR4 P×BP 5 N-QB3 P-N3 6 P-K4 P-Q3 7 N-B3 B-KN2∓ Najdorf-de Miguel, Agrentinian Championship 1960. Once again Black has open lines on the Q-side without being a pawn down.

e) 4 P-QN3? voluntarily opens up the long diagonal and allows Black to open the QN-file. This move has only been seen once in master praxis: 4...P×P 5 P×P P-Q3 6 N-QB3 P-N3 7 B-N2 B-KN2 8 P-B3 QN-Q2 9 P-K4 R-QN1 10 Q-B2 Q-R4 11 K-B2? (better is 11 KN-K2 Q-N5 12 R-QN1 Q×P∓) 11...N×KP+! 12 P×N R×B! 13 Q×R B×N 14 Q-B1 N-B3! 15 N-B3 (if 15 B-Q3 B×R 16 Q×B Q-Q7+ ∓∓ or 15 K-B3 B-KN5+ 16 K-N3 B-K4+ ∓∓) 15...N×KP+ 16 K-K3 B×R 17 Q×B N-B3 18 B-Q3 O-O 19 P-KR3 B-R3 and Black won quickly, Masera-Benko, Reggio Emilia 1971. Now back to the main line.

97

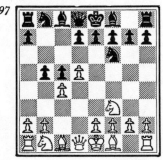

4 ...   B-N2!

Because of the pressure on his QP White will not be able to change his mind and capture the QNP a move or two later than usual.

5 P-KN3

5 P×P? B×P gives Black the advantage at once because of his superior development and central pawn preponderance. Tarasevich-Zaitsev, Moscow 1965, continued 6 N-QB3 B-N2 7 Q-R4 P-Q4 8 N-K5 P-K3 9 N-B6 Q-N3 10 N-R5 QN-Q2 11 P-K3 B-Q3 12 N×B Q×N 13 Q-R6 Q-N1 14 B-K2 O-O. Black's central domination, superior development and more active piece deployment enabled him to crush White without any difficulty.

5 P-QR4 P-QR3 6 RP×P P×P 7 R×R B×R also gives Black an easy game. Kan-Keres, USSR Championship 1955, continued 8 N-B3 and now Black should have played 8...P-N5 with an excellent game, e.g. 9 N-QN5 Q-N3 or 9 Q-R4 P×N 10 Q×B P×P 11 B×P Q-N3.

5 N-QB3 is best met by 5...P-N5 6 Q-N3 Q-N3 with a roughly equal position.

5 ...	P-N3
6 B-N2	B-N2
7 O-O	P-Q3
8 R-K1	P×P
9 P-K4	O-O

Black has many of the typical Benko Gambit advantages without having sacrificed a pawn. The position is roughly equal, with Black having whatever advantage is going. Klaman-Keres, USSR Championship 1957.

15 English Opening

As with the other flank openings 1 N-KB3, 1 P-KN3 and 1 P-QN3, the English Opening is less tangible in many ways than 1 P-Q4 and 1 P-K4. Transpositional possibilities are rife in many of its variations and the order in which some of its moves are played is often of little consequence. It is because of these manifold nuances that the English is often regarded with an apprehensive vagueness by many players. It is not usually thought to be the sort of opening that one can get one's teeth into and the club player who encounters it is usually content to make things up as he goes along.

Here we recommend a system for Black in which he plays to achieve an aggressive set-up from the very start.

           1 P-QB4   P-K4

Already we have arrived at a point of divergence. We shall divide our survey into:

A 2 N-KB3
B 2 P-KN3
C 2 N-QB3

A

1 P-QB4 P-K4

           2 N-KB3(*98*)

This move at once provides Black with a target for his aggressive tendencies!

2 ...	P-K5
3 N-Q4	N-QB3
4 N×N	

4 N-N3 gives Black another opportunity to show his aggressive nature. Chekhover-Kan, USSR 1939, went 4...P-QR4! 5 P-QR4 N-B3 6 N-B3 B-K2 7 P-N3 P-Q4 8 P×P N-QN5 9 B-N2 B-KB4 10 O-O N5×P 11 N×N Q×N∓ with a crushing central superiority for Black.

4 N-B2 is also somewhat passive and against it Fine suggests the following line: 4...P-Q4! 5 P×P Q×P 6 N-B3 Q-K4 7 P-Q4 P×Pep 8 Q×P N-N5 9 N×N B×N 10 Q-B4 B×N+ 11 Q×B Q×Q+ 12 P×Q B-K3. Fine assesses the position as equal but we are of the opinion that Black's chances are slightly the better. Black has a Q-side pawn majority and a lead in development. In addition White's Q-side pawns are weak.

4 P-K3 produces a position akin to the Nimzowitsch Variation of the Sicilian Defence in reverse. After 4... N×N 5 P×N P-Q3 6 N-B3 N-B3 7 P-Q3 P×P 8 B×P B-K2, the position offers chances to both sides.

4 ...	QP×N
5 N-B3	

5 P-QN3 is innocuous: 5...B-KB4 6 B-N2 N-B3 7 P-K3 B-B4 8 B-K2= Pachman. Black has an easy development and White must watch that his backward QP does not become a liability.

5 P-Q4 P×Pep 6 Q×P Q×Q 7 P×Q B-KB4 also produces a balanced position, e.g. 8 B-K3 O-O-O 9 P-Q4 N-B3 10 P-B3 B-QN5+ 11 N-B3 KR-K1 12 K-B2= Tartakower-Alekhine, 1936. Black has the freer development but White's central pawns cannot easily be attacked.

5 ...	N-B3
6 P-K3	

6 P-KN3 B-QB4 7 B-N2 B-B4 8 O-O O-O leaves Black with much the freer game, his pieces already being actively placed.

6 ...	B-KB4
7 P-B3	B-QN5

Black has a fine position — he is two tempi ahead in development and he has a distinct advantage in space.

B

1 P-QB4 P-K4

2 P-KN3	P-Q3
3 B-N2	P-KB4 (*99*)

99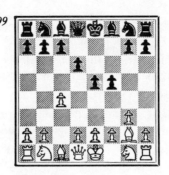

From this diagram the reader can perceive the basis of Black's strategy. The idea is to play a sort of Dutch Defence in which Black has already achieved . . .P-K4 (his thematic break in the Dutch). Behind his aggressive looking pawns Black plans to develop his pieces in readiness for a K-side attack.

4 P-K3

4 N-QB3 or 4 P-Q3 will transpose to variation C.

4 P-Q4 N-KB3 5 P×P P×P 6 Q×Q+ K×Q is not a very ambitious way for White to behave. Tomson-Phillips, World Junior Championship 1959,. continued 7 N-KB3 B-N5+ 8 B-Q2 B×B+ 9 N3×B P-K5 10 N-QB3 B-K3 11 O-O-O K-K2 12 P-B3 P-K6 13 N-B1 B×P 14 N×P B-K3 15 N.K3-Q5+ N×N 16 N×N+ K-B2 17 P-B4 N-R3 with equal chances and an early draw.

4 ...   N-KB3
5 P-Q4

Again 5 N-QB3 or 5 P-Q3 will transpose to variation C.

5 ...   B-K2
6 N-K2

Again 6 P×P P×P 7 Q×Q+ K×Q offers White nothing, e.g. 8 N-QB3 P-B3 9 B-Q2 B-K3 10 P-N3 N-R3 11 O-O-O N-B2 with some advantage to Black (Bobotsov).

6 ...   P-B3

This move represents an important part of Black's strategy in variation C as well as this one. The idea is to deprive White's knight of the use of his Q5 square after he has played QN-B3, to blunt the effect of White's fianchettoed bishop and, in some variations, to prepare for the manoeuvre ...N-R3-B2 with the possibility of an eventual ...N-K3, ...P-KN4 and/or ...P-B5.

7 P-N?   O-O

8 B-N2	QN-Q2
9 QN-B3	Q-K1

This move is characteristic of the Dutch Defence — Black's queen can be put to good use on the K-side either at . . .KR4 or . . .KN3.

10   P-QR4?!

Somewhat inaccurate as it allows Black to get a knight entrenched at . . .QN5. Better would be 10 O-O Q-R4 with chances for both sides.

10 ...	P-QR4
11 B-QR3	N-N1!

Heading for . . .QN5.

12 Q-Q2	N-R3 .
13 O-O-O	

13 O-O is possibly stronger but then Black's position would still offer attacking prospects against White's king.

13 ...	N-QN5
14 P-Q5	P-B4

The practical chances are about even. Ujtelky-Barcza, Budapest 1960, continued 15 P-B3 B-Q2 16 P-K4 (not 16 N-N5 B×N 17 RP×B P-R5! 18 B×N P×B 19 Q×P P×P 20 Q×P.N3 N-Q2! and Black has excellent attacking chances for the pawn) 16...Q-N3 17 KR-N1 N-K1 18 P-B4?! (18 P-R4 B-KB3 19 B-B1 is better, maintaining the balance.) 18...B-KB3 19 K-N1 N-B2 20 B-KB1 QR-K1 21 B-B1 R-K2 22 Q-K1 R1-K1 and Black's strong pressure (especially the rooks) gives him the advantage.

C

1 P-QB4 P-K4

2 N-QB3

This is by far the most usual move.

2 ...   P-Q3

We now consider:

C1 3 P-KN3

C2 3 N-B3

3 P-Q4 P×P 4 Q×P presents Black with a couple of free tempi: 4...N-QB3 5 Q-Q2 N-B3. Lengyel-Barcza, Hungarian Championship 1959, continued 6 P-KN3 B-K2 7 B-N2 O-O 8 P-N3 N-QN5 9 B-N2 P-B3 10 P-K4 (This is just an invitation for Black to open up the position.) 10...P-Q4 11 BP×P P×P 12 P-QR3 P-Q5! 13 N-Q5 N5×N 14 P×N R-K1 15 K-B1 N×P 16 B×P B-N4∓ — the position of White's king will cause him trouble.

3 P-K3 P-KB4 4 P-Q4 B-K2 5 P-B5 accomplishes nothing for White. After 5...N-KB3 6 BP×P BP×P 7 P×P P×P White seems to have sacrificed a couple of tempi to open up the position under circumstances favourable 'to his opponent. Thomas-Beach, British Championship 1958, continued 8 Q-N3 N-B3 9 N-B3 N-K5 10 B-N5 N-B4 11 Q-Q5 Q×Q 12 N×Q B-Q3 13 O-O B-K3 with a fully satisfactory game.

Cl

1 P-QB4 P-K4 2 N-QB3 P-Q3

        3 P-KN3(*100*)

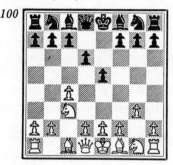

3 ...   P-KB4
4 B-N2

4 P-K4? is completely unthematic. After 4...P×P 5 N×P N-KB3 6 B-N2 N-B3 7 N-K2 B-K2, White's game suffers from various weaknesses; in particular his Q4 and KB3 squares are weak, e.g.
8 P-Q4 N×P 9 N2×N P×N 10 Q×P N×N 11 Q×N O-O   ; or
8 O-O B-N5! 9 P-KR3! B-K3! 10 N×N+ B×N 11 P-Q3 Q-Q2 12 N-B3 O-O-O ∓ Bialas-Schmid, Bamberg 1960. In both cases Black's position is more active.

4 P-K3 is dealt with in the note to White's next move.

4 P-Q4 P-K5 5 P-B3 N-KB3 transposes to the Keres-Levy game which is also mentioned in the next note.

        4 ...   N-KB3
        5 P-Q3

5 P-Q4 P-K5 6 P-B3 P×P was played in Keres-Levy, simultaneous game 1962, which continued 7 N×P B-K2 8 O-O O-O 9 P-Q5 QN-Q2 10 N-Q4 N-K4 11 N×P N×BP 12 P-K4 N-K4 13 B-R3? K-R1 and now, in a position that was already looking good for Black, Keres walked into my cheapo 14 Q-K2? P-KN3 15 B-R6 R-B2 16 R-B4? (or 16 N×B B×B and the knight is trapped) 16...P×N 17 P×P N-N1! and lost quickly. 7

P×P was suggested as an improvement, but then Black has a satisfactory form of Dutch Defence in which he never has need to worry about White's dreaded thrust P-K4.

After 5 P-Q4 P-K5, 6 B-N5 does not seem to have much point. White's bishop exerts no useful pressure along the KR4-Q8 diagonal and it can later be used as a target for the speeding up of Black's attack. Ujtelky-Nezhmetdinov, Rostov 1961, continued 6...B-K2 7 P-K3 O-O 8 KN-K2 Q-K1 9 P-KR4 Q-B2 10 Q-N3 N-R3 11 N-B4 P-B3 (Black had actually played ...P-B3 earlier and only now ...P-Q3 but the transposition is of little significance) 12 B-B1 N-B2 13 P-Q5 N-R3 14 B-K2 N-B4 15 Q-B2 P-KR3 and Black had the initiative.

5 P-K3 is another possibility, preparing for P-Q4 in conjunction with KN-K2 or N-KB3. After 5...B-K2 play might continue 6 KN-K2 P-B3 7 P-Q4 O-O 8 P-N3 (or 8 O-O Q-K1 9 P-B5 P-K5 10 P×P B×P 11 B-Q2 B-K3 12 P-B3 B-B5 13 P×P P×P when White's bishops are too restricted—Djurasevic-Blatny, Lyons 1955) 8 QN-Q2 9 O-O P-KR4 10 P-KR4 N-N5 11 P-B3 N-R3 12 B-QR3 Q-K1 13 P×P P×P 14 B×B Q×B 15 Q-Q2 N-B4 and Black has a minimal space advantage, Gonzales-Rossolimo, Havana 1952.

5 N-R3 was, at one time, a favourite with Forintos. It seems rather difficult to justify putting the knight on such a square, since even if White can coax Black's KP away and then play N-B4, Black's ...P-KN4 will come with gain of tempo on the knight. After 5...P-B3 6 P-Q4 B-K2 7 O-O O-O 8 R-N1 N-R3 9 P-QR3 K-R1, Black has a fine game.

5 N-B3 B-K2 6 O-O P-B3 7 P-Q4 is proved bad by 7 ...P-K5 8 N-K1 because after White's P-B3 P×P; N×P he will be a tempo down on the Keres-Levy game mentioned earlier and in addition Black has played the useful move ...P-B3. In fact White's loss of time is already serious and it is possible that Black can take immediate advantage of this by 8...P-Q4. Fazekas-Fallone, Leicester 1960, continued 9 P×P P×P 10 Q-N3 N-B3 11 B-K3 N-QR4 12 Q-B2 B-Q2∓. After 5 N-B3 B-K2 6 O-O P-B3, White therefore does best to play with restraint, transposing to the text by 7 P-Q3.

5 P-QN4 is yet another possibility, starting the Q-side attack earlier than usual and before Black has had time to complete his development. It would appear that Black still has no need to worry because after 5...P-B3 6 P-N5 he can afford to give away a tempo by 6...P-B4!. The Q-side is now blocked and Black can turn his attention to the other wing where he will be the aggressor. Korchnoi-German, Stockholm Interzonal 1962, continued 7 B-N2 QN-Q2 8 P-Q3 P-KN3 9 P-QR4 P-QR4! 10 P×Pep R×P 11 N-B3 B-N2 12 N-Q2 O-O 13 N-N5 R-B2 14 B-QB3?! N-B1 15 P-K3 N-K3 16 O-O P-KN4! (with an excellent attack)

17 Q-K2 R-K2 18 KR-K1 P-N5 19 P-B4 NP×Pep 20 N×BP N-B1 21 N-Q2 N-N3 22 N-N3 B-R3 23 P-R5 N-N5 24 B-Q5+ K-R1 25 Q-Q2 R-N2 26 K-R1, and now with 26...P-B5! Black's attack would have been sustained (e.g. 27 KP×P N×BP!)

5 ...   B-K2

6 N-B3

The most natural move. 6 Q-B2 is out of place because it is not yet clear where White needs his queen. Filipov-Rivera, Varna 1962, continued 6...P-B3 7 N-B3 O-O 8 O-O K-R1 9 P-Q4 P-K5 10 N-KN5 P-Q4 with a good game for Black.

6 P-K3 represents a different plan to that arising in the note to White's fifth move. White is not playing for the break P-Q4, he is giving his KBP the freedom to advance whenever it will be necessary to forestall Black's ...P-B5. Veto-Lombardy, Leningrad 1960, continued 6...O-O 7 KN-K2 K-R1 8 R-QN1 Q-K1 9 P-QN4 N-B3 10 N-Q5 N×N 11 P×N N-Q1 12 O-O B-Q2 13 P-B4 B-KB3 14 Q-Q2 N-B2 15 P-K4 N-R3, and Black still had attacking prospects on the K-side. The game concluded: 16 B-N2 Q-R4 17 BP×P QP×P 18 B-B1 R-B2 19 N-B3 P-B5 20 B-B3 B-N5 21 Q-KN2 P×P 22 P×P B-N4 23 B.B3×B R×R+ 24 Q×R N×B 25 Q-K2 R-KB1 26 N-Q1 R-B8+ 0-1.

6 P-B4 at once allows Black to open the K-file to his advantage: 6...O-O 7 P-K3 P×P 8 KP×P R-K1 9 KN-K2 P-B3 10 P-Q4 N-R3 11 Q-N3 K-R1 leaves Black's pieces better co-ordinated, van Oosterom-Martens, Leningrad 1960.

6 N-R3 P-B3 7 O-O O-O 8 P-B4 is no better. Golembek-Haygarth. British Championship 1959 continued: 8...N-N5 9 P-K3 B-K3 9 N-B2 N×N 11 R×N N-Q2 12 K-R1 N-B3 13 R-B1 Q-K1∓.

6 ...   O-O

7 O-O(*101*)

7 P-B5 QN-Q2 8 P×P B×P 9 O-O (if 9 N-QN5 B-B4 followed by ...P-B3) 9...P-B3 10 Q-B2 is a fruitless plan, weakening White's control

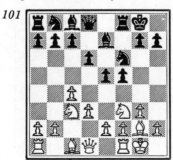

101

of his Q5 square and increasing the scope of Black's KB. Campomanes-
Lagha, Leipzig 1960, continued 10...Q-K2 11 B-N5 P-KR3 12 B-Q2 N-
N3 13 QR-Q1 B-K3 14 N-KR4 Q-KB2 and Black had the more active
game.

| 7 ... | K-R1 |

So that when the tactics start Black will not need to worry about
awkward checks on the light squared diagonal.

8 P-QN4	Q-K1
9 B-N2	Q-R4
10 P-K3	

Otherwise comes 10...N-B3 11 P-QR3 N-Q5!

10 ...	N-B3
11 P-QR3	B-Q2
12 N-Q2	Q-R3

Black has built up excellent attacking prospects against White's K-
side. Hallerod-Hearst, Leningrad 1960, continued 13 N-Q5 N×N 14
P×N N-Q1 15 R-B1 R-B1 16 P-B4 B-KB3 17 N-B4 N-B2 18 P-K4 P-
QN4 19 BP×P QP×P 20 N-R5 B-N4 21 R-QB2 B-K6+ 22 K-R1 P-B5
with a very strong attack. The game concluded: 23 P×P B×P 24 B-KB3
Q-R6 25 B-B1 N-N4 26 B×B R×B 27 B-N2 Q-R5 28 N-B6 B×N 29 R×B
R1-B1 30 R×R P×R 31 R×P P-B6 32 B×P Q-B5 33 R-B2 N×B 34 R-B2
P-N4 35 P-Q6 P-N5 36 Q-R1+ K-N1 37 P-K5 R-B1 38 Q-R2+ K-N2 39
R-B2 Q-Q5 0-1.

The reader will have noticed throughout his study of this variation
that Black frequently acquires an active position by means of a series of
almost stereotyped moves. This ease with which the repertoire player
can put his plan into practice should make our recommendation all the
more attractive.

C2

1 P-QB4 P-K4 2 N-QB3 P-Q3

3 N-B3 *(102)*

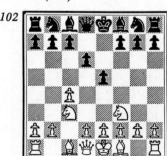

3 ...	P-KB4
4 P-Q4	

4 P-K4 unnecessarily weakens White's Q4 square. A 1959 correspondence game, Mozulevsky-Marini, went 4...N-KB3 5 P-Q3 N-B3 6 B-K2 B-K2 7 O-O O-O 8 N-K1 N-Q5 9 P-B4 P-B3∓. White cannot imitate his opponent's hold on Q5.

4 P-KN3 N-KB3 5 P-Q3 will transpose to variation B.

4 ...	P-K5
5 N-N5	

5 N-Q2 has been played on a few occasions, notably in the game Boleslavsky-Bronstein from the 1953 Candidates tournament at Zurich. White intends to break up the centre with P-B3 but Black can hinder this plan by ...P-KN3 and ...B-R3 with good play on the dark squares. The game continued 5...P-B3 6 P-K3 N-KB3 7 B-K2 (if 7 P-B3 at once, Black can take the initiative with 7...P×P 8 Q×P P-KN3! 9 B-Q3 B-N2 10 P-K4 O-O! 11 P×P N-K1∓ and both White's queen and QP are exposed, Schmid-Nilsson, Stockholm 1965-6) 7...P-KN3 8 O-O B-R3 9 P-QN4 O-O 10 P-N5 R-K1 with equal chances.

5 N-N1 transposes to the text after 5...B-K2 6 N-R3.

5 ...	B-K2
6 N-KR3	

6 P-KR4 is adorned with an exclamation mark by Schwarz but it seems that it is only justified if Black plays ...P-KR3 allowing N-R3-B4. Instead Black should simply continue with his development: Naranja-Tan, Leipzig 1960, went 6...N-KB3 7 B-B4?! N-R4! 8 N-R3 N×B 9 N×N P-K6! 10 P-KN3 P×P+ 11 K×P P-B3 and White had nothing to show for his weakened king position.

6 ...	P-B3!
7 P-KN3	

7 P-K3 N-B3 8 B-K2 N-R3 9 O-O N-B2 10 P-B3 is possibly a better plan. After 10...O-O White should not play 11 P-Q5? because of 11...BP×P 12 P×QP P×P 13 B×P N-Q2, when Black has the use of his beautiful K4 square (±). Instead White should play 11 B-Q2, and after 11...R-N1! 12 P-QN4 P-QN4 Black's advantage is not so pronounced.

7 ...	N-B3
8 N-B4	O-O
9 P-KR4	

Otherwise ...P-KN4 will soon appear on the horizon.

9 ...	N-R3
10 P-K3	N-B2

11 B-Q2	K-R1
12 Q-B2	B-Q2 ±

Black's pieces are harmoniously developed and White's K-side is full of holes. Pachman-Matanovic, Portoroz interzonal 1958.

16 N-KB3

Old Indian Defence (Tartakower Variation)

	1 N-KB3	P-Q3
	2 P-Q4	

2 P-B4 transposes to the English, 2 P-K4 to the Pirc/Modern.

	2 ...	B-N5(*103*)

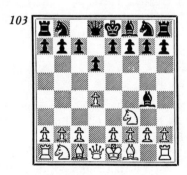

103

A favourite move of the Polish grandmaster Savielly Tartakower and of one of the co-authors, Raymond Keene, this comparatively rare line takes us out of normal 'theory'. If now 3 P-K4, a Modern Defence position can arise if Black fianchettos his KB.

        3 P-B4

3 P-KR3? is a waste of a move which forces Black into 3...BxN, a move he intended anyway.

The game M. Fuller-Keene, British Championship, Coventry 1970, continued 3 P-KR3 BxN 4 NPxB N-Q2 5 B-N2 KN-B3 6 P-KB4 (bringing his KB to life; Black at once takes steps to block the diagonal) 6...P-Q4 7 P-B4 P-B3 8 N-B3 N-N3 9 PxP PxP 10 Q-N3 P-K3 11 P-QR4 P-QR4 12 P-B5 B-N5 13 PxP PxP 14 O-O (note that Black's surrender of bishop for knight has weakened White's king position-a factor Black exploits in subsequent play.) 14...O-O 15 P-K4 B×N 16 P×B N×KP 17 R-N1 R-R3 18 P-QB4 Q-R5! 19 B-R3 R-B3 20 P×P N×QP 21 Q×P P-R3‼ (Offering a rook for fantastic complications – White has to weather a furious combinative storm.) 22 Q×R R-N3 23 R-N3 (White misses a probable draw here: 23 Q-B8+ K-R2 24 Q-B2 N-B5 25 Q×N N×P+ 26 K-R2 N-B5+ etc.) 23...Q-N4 24 R-N3 N×R 25 P×N Q×P 26 R-B8+ K-R2 27 Q-K2 Q×B.R6 and with a strong attack plus an extra pawn Black soon won.

3 ...   B×N

Black exchanges bishop for knight to double White's KBP. White's pawn structure now becomes more cumbersome, but as compensation he possesses the bishop pair. The position has thus been 'unbalanced' very efficiently.

4 NP×B

4 KP×B offers White fewer possibilities. While he can operate on a semi-open K-file in place of a KN-file, the capture away from the centre gives up the chance to create a central pawn mass. Furthermore, White cannot quickly post his KB actively on the long diagonal by B-KN2 as he can after 4 NP×B. A similar set-up would have arisen after 3 P-KN3, answered by 3...B×N!

4 ...   N-KB3
5 N-B3

5 Q-N3 is answered simply by 5...Q-B1. Appel-Tartakower, Lodz 1938, continued 6 P-B4 P-KN3 7 B-N2 P-B3 8 N-Q2 (8 P-K4 B-N2 9 P-K5 N3-Q2 10 P×P P×P 11 Q-K3+ K-Q1 12 O-O R-K1 13 Q-Q3 P-KB4 – 'unclear', Tartakower) 8...B-N2 9 O-O O-O 10 N-B3 QN-Q2 11 B-K3 P-K3 12 QR-B1 R-Q1 with a sound position for Black. 5 B-N2 or P-K4 or P-B4 will all probably transpose to the game we are following. However, if 5 B-N5, Black must take care to play QN-Q2 at once to avoid the doubling of his KB pawn.

5 ...   P-KN3

Black can now continue his plan of development against virtually any of White's possible piece-developments; e.g.,

6 P-K4	P-B3
7 B-K3	P-K3
8 P-B4	QN-Q2
9 B-N2	Q-B2
10 O-O	B-K2(104)

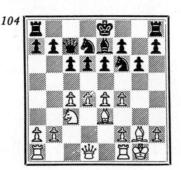

Black is well poised to hold any White advances in the centre or on either wing. He has a very sound position and has completed his development. Kluger-Petrosian, Leipzig 1960, continued 11 R-B1 O-O 12 K-R1 N-R4 13 P-KB5 KP×P 14 P×P N2-B3 15 R-KN! K-R1 16 Q-B3 QR-K1 17 P-N4 N-N2 with a very complex position. Black won.

17 Nimzowitsch-Larsen Attack — 1 P-QN3

This is an opening which was first popularized at international level by grandmaster Aaron Nimzowitsch in the 1920s. Subsequently Bent Larsen adopted it in an attempt to avoid well analyzed openings where thinking becomes automatic, such as certain lines of the Lopez or the Sicilian. It gained complete respectability when Fischer used it to defeat Filip and Mecking in the 1970 Interzonal.

1 P-QN3   P-K4(*105*)

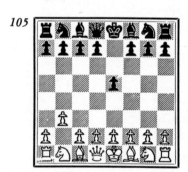

105

  This is a sound and aggressive pawn move which occupies the centre while limiting the scope of White's QB on the long diagonal.

2 B-N2

The only logical reply.

2 ...   N-QB3

Defending the KP while developing the QN.

3 P-QB4

  This is considered White's most important move. Against 3 P-KN3 or 3 P-Q3 3...P-Q4 will more than equalize for Black. Black has a good pawn centre and excellent piece development. If 3 P-K3, however, not 3...P-Q4 because of 4 B-QN5 with initiative, but 3...P-Q3 as in the text.

3 ...	N-B3

More solid development.

4 P-K3

If 4 P-KN3 Black can continue his development with . . . P-Q3, . . . P-KN3 and . . . B-N2. 4 N-KB3? is a move which has been regarded with a jaundiced eye ever since Larsen-Spassky, Belgrade 1970. That game continued 4...P-K5! 5 N-Q4 B-B4 6 NxN QPxN 7 P-K3 B-B4 8 Q-B2 Q-K2 9 B-K2 O-O-O and with his harmonious development and pressure in the centre, Black had the better of it. The game concluded drastically 10 P-B4 N-N5 11 P-N3 P-KR4 12 P-KR3 P-R5 13 PxN PxP 14 R-N1 R-R8 15 RxR P-N7 16 R-B1 Q-R5+ 17 K-Q1 PxR=Q+ 0-1.

4 ...	P-Q3
5 N-QB3é	

If 5 P-Q4, 5...B-KB4 as occurs later in the line we are following.

5 ...	P-KN3
6 N-B3	B-N2
7 P-Q4	

If 7 B-K2, of course simply 7...O-O.

7 ...	B-B4

As in Larsen-Portisch, Siegen 1970. Once again Black's development is harmonious and he has an equal share of the centre. Larsen continued:

8 P-Q5	N-QN5
9 R-B1	P-QR4

To prevent P-QN4 after . . . N-R3 and . . . N-B4.

10 P-QR3	N-R3
11 P-R3	O-O

The chances are even after 12 B-K2 N-B4 13 O-O. In the game Larsen continued riskily with 12 P-KN4? which led to another quick finish:
12...B-Q2 13 P-N5 N-R4 14 N-K4 P-KB4 15 PxPep NxP 16 N3-Q2 NxN 17 NxN Q-R5 18 N-N3 N-B4 19 B-B3? RxP 20 KxR N-K5+ 21 K-N1 QxN+ 22 B-N2 QxP+ 0-1.

18 Reti-Benko Opening — 1 P-KN3

This opening is very much of a byway since it will normally transpose to the English. White's obvious intention after P-KN3 is to exert pressure down the long light-square diagonal and usually the move P-QB4 would support this.

| 1 P-KN3 | P-K4 |

A sound pawn move like this must always be good.

| 2 B-N2 |

If 2 P-QB4 we have an English, and after 2 P-QN3 we are back to the Nimzowitsch-Larsen attack, 2 N-KB3 is an interesting attempt to play a reversed Alekhine's Defence with an extra move (1 P-KN3), 2...P-K5 3 N-Q4, as in Larsen-Donner, Zurich 1959, just weakens Black's centre so 2...N-QB3 is the best reply. Then 3 P-B4 is an English again, 3 P-Q3 transposes back to the main line, and 3 B-N2 P-K5 is obviously good for Black since White's KN can no longer advance and must beat the dismal retreat back to KN1.

| 2 ... | N-QB3(*106*) |

106

White has spent his first two moves accomplishing little more than the development of one bishop. Black, on the other hand, already has a strong central position and potential for comfortable, direct development.

3 P-Q3   P-B4

An aggressive move with twin points: (1) influence on the centre and (2) creation of possibilities of K-side attack for Black. Black's KBP can later advance to ...KB5 to take advantage of White's target pawn on KN3 or support a central thrust via ...P-K5.

4 N-KB3

A transposition to the English can still occur with 4 P-QB4.

4 ...   N-B3

Logical and strong. The second knight bears down on the important central squares.

5 O-O   B-K2
6 P-B3   P-QR4

Black prevents White's space-gaining operation P-QN4. Considering his solid centre he can afford to improve his position slowly forestalling White's attempts at counterplay.

7 P-QR4

7 P-Q4 is an attempt to challenge Black in the centre, but it will fail after 7...P-K5 8 N3-Q2 P-Q4 and White will find it very hard to continue with the thematic P-QB4 in view of the resulting weakness of his QP.

7 ...   O-O

Furthering our sound development and preparing for action with the king safely tucked away and the KR ready for action.

8 N-R3   P-Q4!

Now Black has a fine game since White can no longer undermine his centre efficiently with P-QB4. This advance would leave him with weak squares at QN4 and QB5 inviting occupation by black knights.

A typical continuation could be 9 N-QN5 P-K5 10 N3-Q4 N×N 11 P×N P-B3 12 N-B3 B-K3 13 B-B4 B-Q3 14 B-K5 Q-B2 15 B×B Q×B 16 Q-Q2 and Black has a good position.

19 Bird's Opening – 1 P-KB4

This old debut is occasionally employed by Larsen, but that is about all that can be said in its favour. Black has a wide choice of plans – the repertoire player is recommended one whose quick and easy development will be combined with early attacking possibilities if White does not play accurately.

1 P-KB4   P-Q4(107)

2 N-KB3

The only consistent move, increasing White's grip on the K5 square. Against other moves Black has a very free hand in the centre, e.g. 2 P-QN3 N-KB3 3 B-N2 P-Q5! 4 N-KB3 P-B4$\mp$; or 2 P-KN3 Q-Q3 3 B-N2 (or 3 N-KB3 P-KB3 4 P-Q4 N-B3 5 P-K3 P-K4!) 3...P-K4!

2 ...   N-KB3
3 P-K3   B-N5!

Already Black's position is becoming active. His plan is to force the break ...P-K4, castle Q-side and then launch an attack against White's king.

4 B-K2

If 4 P-KR3 B×N 5 Q×B QN-Q2, White must play 6 P-Q4 (in order to prevent 6...P-K4) and Black is then able to sit a knight on . . .K5 to good effect, e.g. 6 P-Q4 N-K5 7 N-Q2 P-KB4 8 N×N QP×N 9 Q-B2 P-

K3 10 B-B4 Q-B3=.

4 P-QN3 P-KN3 5 B-K2 B-N2 6 B-N2 P-B3 7 O-O O-O also produces a balanced position.

4 ...	B×N
5 B×B	QN-Q2
6 P-Q4	

Black must prevent . . .P-K4 at all costs. An amusing example of the sort of thing that can happen to him if he forgets to do this, is the game Wyss-Barcza, Lugano 1968: 6 P-QN3 P-K4 7 P×P N×P 8 O-O B-Q3 9 B-N2 P-B3 10 P-Q3 Q-B2 11 P-KR3 P-KR4 12 N-Q2 N4-N5 13 B.N2×N B-R7+ 14 K-R1 B-N8 O-1.

6 ...	P-K3
7 O-O	P-B3=

Reti-Kaufmann, Vienna 1914. Black might well continue with ...Q-B2, . . .O-O-O, . . .P-KR3 and . . .P-KN4 with good attacking prospects.